DEDICATION

To Happy Henry Hird—the unofficial mayor of St. Augustine.

When visiting St. Augustine, one must stop and smell the flowers.

100 THINGS TO DO IN ST. AUGUSTINE BEFORE YOU DIE

AMY ANGELILLI

Reedy Press
PO Box 5131
St. Louis, MO 63139, USA
www.reedypress.com

Library of Congress Control Number: 2023951918

ISBN: 9781681065212

Design by Jill Halpin

Printed in the United States of America
24 25 26 27 28   5 4 3 2 1

100 THINGS TO DO IN ST. AUGUSTINE BEFORE YOU DIE

The St. Augustine Lighthouse shines a light on the nation's oldest port.

CONTENTS

Music and Entertainment

Sports and Recreation

Culture and History

Shopping and Fashion

ACKNOWLEDGMENTS

Thank you to the team at visitstaugustine.com—it's a pleasure to spend time in St. Augustine's historic downtown with you discussing what's new, what's old, and what punctuation to use when writing about both. Without you I would not have had the opportunity to write this book, take a deeper dive into St. Augustine, or learn to love St. Augustine Distillery gin. I'm thankful for all three—especially that last one.

PREFACE

When I moved to St. Augustine in 2015, many of my city friends responded with "St. *What*?" Gone are the days of St. Augustine being an under-the-radar, sweet, southern, seaside community. That same year St. Augustine celebrated its 450th anniversary, putting it on the international map. Since then, the town has continued receiving accolades. Here are just a few examples from the list that Florida's Historic Coast maintains:

Budget Travel (May 2023)—The editors named St. Augustine one of the Top 10 Coolest Small Towns in 2023.

Fodor's Travel (May 2023)—The editors named St. Augustine one of the 15 Most Romantic Small Towns across the United States.

Woman's World (May 2023)—St. Augustine took the number one spot in the South's Eight Sweetest Cities list.

Southern Living (March 2023)—The South's Best Awards, featuring St. Augustine as the Best Small Town in the South.

USA Today 10 Best (March 2023)—*USA Today* readers named St. Augustine a Top 10 Small Town in the US.

msn.com (August 2022)—St. Augustine recognized as number three on the 30 Most Beautiful Small Towns and Cities in Florida list.

Lonely Planet (June 2022)—St. Augustine included on the list of the 10 Most Storied Places in the US to Visit in 2022.

Conde Nast Traveler (December 2021)—St. Augustine took the number one slot on the list of US Cities That Are Full of European Charm.

BeChewy.com (June 2021)—Named St. Augustine number six on the Top 10 Best Dog-Friendly Vacation Destinations for 2021. (Even the dogs love it here!)

Sharing St. Augustine with you is bittersweet for me. Part of me wants to keep it all to myself (if that were even possible). And part of me wants to shout from the historic rooftops, "Yes, I do live in the prettiest town in America—thank you very much! Come see for yourself." With St. Augustine continuing to grow and evolve, there's no way to keep it a secret anymore, so welcome. Welcome to my adopted hometown. May you love it as much as I do.

And one more thing . . . it was nearly impossible to narrow the list to only 100 entries. With St. Augustine now a world-class destination, this is merely a jumping-off point as the culinary, art, music, craft beer, maker, and entrepreneurial communities continue blooming. Keep in touch with St. Augustine's "100 Things" on Facebook and Instagram @100thingsstaugustine—and don't forget to tag your own #100ThingsStAugustine adventures while you're there.

Viva San Agustin!

—Amy Angelilli

Cool off with a craft cocktail in historic downtown St. Augustine.

FOOD AND DRINK

1

VIVA THE CRAFT COCKTAIL REVOLUTION
IN SAN AGUSTIN

Distillers have been creating spirits in St. Augustine for centuries. Pedro Menéndez brought a brewmaster with him when he arrived from Spain in 1565, and the town's namesake, St. Augustine of Hippo, is the patron saint of brewers. More recently, the town has been captivated by fancy spirits. Craft alcohol made with love and care—usually in small batches—allows for a higher degree of quality control and a greater emphasis on flavor. See how local spirits are made and enjoy the best possible version of a cocktail classic. St. Augustine is the oldest—and finest—city for top-notch drinking endeavors.

The St. Augustine Distillery leads the number one whiskey tour in the United States. Take the tour, sample the goods, then go next door to the Ice Plant for cocktails made from the distillery spirits and enjoy one of the best menus in town, too.

St. Augustine Distillery
112 Riberia St., 904-825-4962
staugustinedistillery.com

Ice Plant Bar and Restaurant
110 Riberia St., 904-829-6553
iceplantbar.com

OTHER FINE ESTABLISHMENTS TO ENJOY A CRAFT COCKTAIL

Casa Reina Taqueria & Tequila
1 Anderson Cir., 904-295-3847
casareinastaug.com

The Floridian
72 Spanish St., 904-829-0655
thefloridianstaug.com

Forgotten Tonic
6 Aviles St., 904-827-9055
forgottentonic.com

Odd Birds Cocktail Lounge & Kitchen
200 Anastasia Blvd., 904-342-8378
oddbirdsbar.com

2

SPORT A VINTAGE BATHING SUIT AT CAFÉ ALCAZAR

Café Alcazar is one of St. Augustine's most unique places to eat, located in what used to be the Hotel Alcazar swimming pool—the largest in the world during its heyday. Situated behind the Lightner Museum, the café is a white-tablecloth lunchtime dining experience. Henry Flagler built the Alcazar Hotel and Casino, now known as the Lightner Museum, in 1888. (Yes, that Henry Flagler—the one Flagler College is named after. The college is only a short walk from the café.)

The café is almost hidden in the deep end of the old pool, with antique-filled shops surrounding it. In the wintertime, the "pool" is part café and part event space for festive gatherings such as the annual holiday market. No matter what time of year it is, Café Alcazar is a hidden gem that both locals and visitors enjoy.

25 Granada St., 904-825-9948
lightnermuseum.org/cafe

3

FEAST ON AWARD-WINNING MEALS
AT LLAMA AND AT MICHAEL'S

Winner of Open Table's 2022 Diners' Choice award, Llama Restaurant has been named one of the top 100 restaurants in the country. A Peruvian native, Chef Marcel incorporates locally sourced ingredients into his culinary creations. He has also partnered with St. Augustine's Micro Greens to grow exotic Peruvian produce for his dishes in order to offer new culinary experiences.

Over the years, Chef Michael and his historic downtown restaurant of the same name have received numerous honors and accolades. For 11 years in a row, *Wine Spectator* has awarded Michael's wine list its Award of Excellence. Chef Michael has also been recognized as St. Augustine's Best Chef by several city publications. The restaurant was featured on the Food Network with Chef Emeril Lagasse during Viva Florida 500.

Enjoy the magic of both places—just make sure to rest in between.

Llama Restaurant
415 Anastasia Blvd., 904-819-1760
llamarestaurant.com

Michael's
25 Cuna St., 904-810-2400
michaelssa.com

ENJOY OLD-WORLD DINING
AT GAUFRE'S & GOODS

A family-owned-and-operated Polish and Greek café offering traditional dishes in a quaint, intimate nook, Gaufre's & Goods is easy to miss. Many locals are happy about that, as Gaufre's is considered a "secret spot" for those in the know. The menu offers Eastern European beer and wine as well as coffees, waffles, pastries, pierogies, spinach pie, mussels, soups, salads, and daily specials. The dining area is like Grandma's house filled with old things that make it feel like mealtime with European ancestors.

Speaking from experience, it's easy to get carried away with Gaufre's menu. If that's the case, consider two visits—one for the Polish deep dive, and the other for the Greek feast. Whatever the case, do try some Polish pierogies (the house special) and enjoy the Greek baklava (even if it's to take away), as they are very serious about their baklava (the Greek dessert of champions)—as in seriously good.

212 Charlotte St., 904-829-5770

Located on Charlotte Street, Gaufre's is accessible via an alleyway from St. Augustine's oldest street, Aviles Street. Enjoy alfresco dining and then wander through the First Friday Artwalk on Aviles Street. Why eat before the walk? Gaufre's is primarily a lunch spot—except on Saturdays.

5

BE PART OF A FISHING TOWN

WITH A DRINKING PROBLEM AT LOCAL BREWERIES

It used to be said that St. Augustine was a fishing town with a drinking problem. Today, the fish continue to bite, and the craft brew scene is thriving. That means folks have better beer to drink on and off their fishing boats. Enjoy the craft breweries—no fishing required—anytime.

One fun way to do so during the winter holiday season is with Nights of Pints. One fee gets you a Nights of Pints T-shirt and a punch card for a beer from each participating brewery. Every year the event benefits a different local nonprofit organization.

If you're not visiting during the holiday season, no worries. The beer tastes just as good. To have an official tasting with a guide, a snack, and up to 12 beers, try the St. Augustine Craft Beer & History Experience, which offers daily tasting tours at 2 p.m. Or go on your own and visit a different brewery each day, chat with the locals, and pick up some great souvenirs—beer-related, of course.

TIP

Ancient City Brewing has a resident cat named Galleon after Galleon's Golden Ale. Because the brewery is dog-friendly too, it can be a fun place for animal lovers—if Galleon is in a good mood that day!

Nights of Pints
visitstaugustine.com/event/nights-pints

St. Augustine Craft Beer & History Experience
904-599-7432
staugustineexperiences.com/tour/ale-trail-craft-beer-tour

Ancient City Brewing Taproom
18 Cathedral Pl., 904-217-3278

Ancient City Brewhouse
3420 Agricultural Center Dr., 904-429-9654
ancientcitybrewing.com

Bog Brewing Company
218 W King St., 904-679-3146
bogbrewery.com

Dog Rose Brewing Co.
77 Bridge St., 904-217-3355
dogrosebrewing.com

Old Coast Ales
300 Anastasia Blvd., 904-484-7705
oldcoastales.com

6

CHANNEL JAMES BOND
AT TINI MARTINI

The Tini Martini Bar, at the Casablanca Inn on the Bay in St. Augustine's historic downtown, is in a category all its own. Why? First, it (obviously) specializes in martinis, so expect to see some James Bond types. Second, it's haunted. Yup, the ghost hunters have been very busy communicating with the hotel's undead over the years. Third, it's right on the bayfront, so the views are gorgeous. (Google hurricane images of St. Augustine and one of the first photos that pop up is someone kayaking down the street—yes, the street—in front of Tini Martini.) Finally, there is no better-decorated establishment during the holiday season's Nights of Lights than Tini Martini. There's often live jazz or blues, so wear some sparkles and imagine sitting with Bond, James Bond, while sipping martinis.

Tini Martini at the Casablanca Inn
24 Avenida Menendez, 904-829-6099
casablancainn.com/martini-bar

7

EXPERIENCE A SLICE OF THE CARIBBEAN
AT THE CONCH HOUSE

For more than 70 years the Ponce family has owned and operated the Conch House. The Ponces are one of the oldest families in the United States—they've been in St. Augustine for more than 400 years! They used to run the Old Dutch Tavern, which looked like a Dutch windmill. (A photo of the tavern is hanging in the captain's room bar at the Conch House.) Located just next to the Bridge of Lions, "The Tavern" was the place to be according to old-timers, probably because it started as a gambling house. Starting as a four-room hotel called Ponces by the Sea, the Conch House has been using the same family fried-shrimp recipe for three generations. The place is known as "St. Augustine's Caribbean" because of the island-style cuisine and the Jamaican-inspired grass hut that looms over the water.

Conch House Marina Resort
57 Comares Ave., 904-829-8646
conchhousemarinaresort.com

8

CURB YOUR CRAVING FOR FRESH AND LOCAL

AT CRAVE

This may sound silly, but trust me when I say you will crave Crave. What started out as a food truck parked alongside the Sebastian River is now a brick-and-mortar restaurant in historic downtown. While Crave is known for its fresh and healthy wraps, salads, smoothies, and bowls, it's also known for big breakfast and lunch tastes—especially when it comes to the build-your-own salads, wraps, and bowls.

The folks at Crave believe food should be "healthy, local, and fun," and the locals applaud that effort. With dishes including the "Crave-urrito" and smoothies called "So Matcha Love" or my favorite, the "Funky Monkey," Crave delivers the fun daily. And not just in a dish or cup, as fun can be found on the murals in and outside of the building, with the bikes for loan in the parking lot, and with the darling dog that serves as the Crave mascot.

One of the Crave murals reads, "Eat healthy. Feel good." It's the truth. You'll feel great with a morning or afternoon pit stop at Crave.

135 King St., 904-293-6373
cravestaug.com

9

INDULGE IN GOURMET GRILLED CHEESES AND CRAFT BEER

AT SARBEZ

It's hard to describe or classify Sarbez. Some people know it as a gourmet grilled-cheese restaurant. Some people know it as a live-music venue (national touring bands make pit stops here) with a great craft beer selection (25 on tap plus cans and bottles). Still others know it for the 35 arcade games from the '80s ranging from pinball to Skee-Ball. (Yes, there's a quarter machine.) It's also known for its outdoor patio and bonfires. And it showcases local painters and illustrators in the space. Plus, it's family friendly until 8 p.m. (It's open until at least midnight for everyone else.) It's as if someone sat down and posed the question, "What would make the greatest number of people happy?" The answer of course is grilled cheese, craft beer, live music, and arcade games under one roof. Well done!

115 Anastasia Blvd., 904-342-0632
facebook.com/theplanetsarbez

10

SCREAM FOR ICE CREAM

AT MAYDAY HANDCRAFTED ICE CREAMS

Artisan, homemade ice cream made right here in St. Augustine. And let's not forget the homemade cookie and sprinkles on top! The folks at Mayday believe that "good cold ice cream should make hearts feel warm." And it does . . . especially after discovering that Mayday ice cream can be mailed home. Read that again: it can be mailed anywhere in the United States! Innovative, authentic ice cream made from scratch with love that can be enjoyed in three St. Augustine locations—or at home—delivers smiles every time. Fun flavors include coffee + donuts, blueberry toast crunch, and Key lime pie. There are usually about two dozen flavors available, a half dozen of which are seasonal. This is life-changing ice cream served with old-world hospitality.

Downtown: 100 St. George St., Ste. J, 904-217-0517
St. Augustine Beach: 461 A1A Beach Blvd., 904-342-2593
Midtown: 1765 Tree Blvd., Ste. 5, 904-342-7816
maydayicecream.com

11

DISCOVER WHIMSICAL AND WONDERFUL HANDMADE ICE POPS

AT THE HYPPO

Welcome to the whimsical world of one-of-a-kind handmade ice pops. The Hyppo's delightful all-natural ice pops are literally made with everything under the sun, as there are *more than 450 flavors available*! The base for most of the pops is pure fruit—finally, a way that parents can get the appropriate amount of fruit into their kids! And as the seasons change, the flavors do too—think summer watermelon blueberry to fall pumpkin pie to winter whiskey maple pecan to lavender lemon crème in the spring. And then there are the datil pepper pops. Datil peppers are one of the most popular—and one of the hottest—locally grown products in St. Augustine. The Hyppo has an online store, so the 450-plus flavors can be enjoyed nationwide!

48 Charlotte St., 904-217-7853 (ice pops made here)
70 St. George St., 904-547-2980
thehyppo.com

12

DISCOVER A NOT-SO-SECRET GARDEN
AT CASA DE VINO 57

Sometimes there's great wine, food, and music in a not-so-great setting. Sometimes there's the opposite. And then there's Casa de Vino 57, which has great wine, food, and music in a *fabulous* setting. The folks at Casa de Vino 57 should make wine lovers say a secret passcode to get in—that's how special the secluded courtyard is, even though it's in the middle of historic downtown. From Treasury Street, which by the way is the country's narrowest street, Casa de Vino 57 looks like a historic house. And it is—the Joaneda House was constructed in 1807. Juan Joaneda, who was a wealthy fish farmer and landholder from Minorca, was one of the first immigrants to build homes and flip properties for profit. Today, the Joaneda House is home to boutique wines, charcuterie boards, and cheeses from around the world. Cheers to that!

57 Treasury St., 904-217-4546
casadevino57.com

13

MARRY WAFFLES AND MILKSHAKES

AT COUSTEAU'S WAFFLE & MILKSHAKE BAR

Cousteau's Waffle & Milkshake Bar says that "one great waffle can change the world." Most people with a sweet tooth would say, "One great waffle and a milkshake can change the world," because a milkshake should never be an afterthought! Located in historic downtown, Cousteau's Waffle & Milkshake Bar is the *perfect* pit stop on a hot day because of their Belgian liege waffles and hand-spun milkshakes.

The waffles are made in-house from dough filled with Belgian pearl sugar, then cooked and caramelized on the hot cast-iron press. The milkshakes begin with homemade soft-serve ice cream, which is blended with goodies and topped with whipped cream. The made-to-order waffles and milkshakes can be eaten separately or together. Imagine dipping a waffle specialty into a milkshake of choice. It's a good thing downtown is pedestrian friendly, as a long walk after visiting Costeau's is recommended.

Cousteau's Downtown
15 Hypolita St., 904-342-5627
wafflemilk.com

Cousteau's Beachside
3920 SR-A1A S

14

MOVE ABOUT THE CABIN

AT HANGAR ONE BISTRO

It's rare to *want* to visit an airport. However, the sweet little airport in St. Augustine is not only a pleasant experience, it's one that doesn't even require a plane ticket to enjoy. Hangar One Bistro is a combination of delicious dining, beautiful cocktails, and fabulous views. With two climate-controlled indoor patios, diners can enjoy watching the main runways, the airport taxiways, and the aircraft parking areas—all with the Intracoastal Waterway as a gorgeous backdrop.

Considered an aviation dining experience, Hangar One Bistro serves dinner and weekend brunch so diners can get a good look at the runway under the sun—and under the stars. The European and Latin American–inspired menu is perfect for the space, as these dishes are meant to be savored, not rushed. And since there's no flight to catch, there's no reason not to linger.

Northeast Florida Regional Airport at 4900 US-1 N, 904-602-6003
hangaronebistro.com

DIVE INTO A VEGGIE DISH
AT MANATEE CAFE

The café has been a St. Augustine staple for more than 25 years, serving vegetarian and vegan dishes made with organically grown fruits, vegetables, legumes, grains, and herbs. The dishes are healthy, and they taste a-ma-zing, which is why literally *everyone* loves the Manatee Cafe. Now about those manatees . . . the café is decorated with local art (for sale) that's all about the Florida manatee. Enjoy a fabulously healthy meal and take home a manatee. Win–win!

This breakfast and lunch staple also has a little shopping nook featuring homemade bread, organic coffee, vitamin supplements, and natural beauty products. And since the café is so entrenched in the community, it has the best community bulletin board in town, so diners always know what's happening around St. Augustine, too!

525 FL-16, #106, 904-826-0210
manateecafe.com

TOUR THE TOWN
VIA LOCAL FOOD TRUCK PARKS

The food truck fad is here to stay—making it not a fad at all, but a gift from the gods. In St. Augustine there's not one but two food truck parks—one on the water and one in a green space.

Marina Munch, at English Landing Marina, has salty breezes, gorgeous views, and several trucks—some anchor, some visitor—seven days a week for lunch and dinner. The anchor, Uptown Scratch Kitchen, is a favorite and for good reason—the rosemary garlic fries can't be beat.

The Village Garden is a little green playground for all ages on Anastasia Island. The garden perimeter houses the trucks while the interior is home to lawn games. It's a place to eat, drink, and be merry—literally. It's also open seven days a week, and because it has a café, the party starts in the morning with fresh coffee.

Marina Munch
English Landing Marina, 509 S Ponce De Leon Blvd., 904-315-7454

Village Garden Food Truck Park
1480 S Old A1A S, 904-217-8488
villagegardenftp.com

SOAK IN THE SCENERY
AT THE REEF RESTAURANT

According to the Reef Restaurant's website, it's "one of the most spectacular oceanfront settings in Northeast Florida." The locals, the visitors, and the motorists along A1A would all agree with this sentiment. The restaurant, perched high atop the dune, overlooks the tide, so diners can sometimes be spellbound watching it roll in and out—especially if they happen to be drinking a local beer while they watch. For more than 20 years, this family-owned-and-operated restaurant has been serving lunch, dinner, and Sunday brunch on tables inside and out—all with beautiful ocean views. Diners can eat local while enjoying the scenery as the Reef serves a fresh catch of the day and several dishes with the famously spicy St. Augustine datil pepper. The hard part is leaving—but at least the drive back to town is gorgeous.

4100 Coastal Hwy., 904-824-8008
thereefstaugustine.com

SOAK UP THE SALAD DRESSING
AT GYPSY CAB COMPANY

Celebrating more than 40 years in business, Gypsy Cab Company brought urban cuisine to St. Augustine when it first opened in the early 1980s. Painted in a New York City taxi motif, Gypsy Cab has Mediterranean, Italian, German, Caribbean, Cajun, Southern, Asian, and "Floribbean" influences. And yet, despite these influences, the locals will tell you to go for the simple Gypsy House Salad. Why? Because it's huge, the croutons are made in-house, and it's served with Gypsy's famous dressing.

The regular menu, known as "Cab Fare," is popular with locals, who can be found sitting at the bar discussing the day's news. The specials menu changes seasonally to highlight what the local farmers are growing, making for some fun scratch items. Owner Frank O'Rourke speaks the truth when he says Gypsy's menu is a blend of a lot of different influences. Cheers to that!

828 Anastasia Blvd., 904-824-8244
gypsycab.com

Gypsy's homemade salad dressing has become so popular over the years that it's bottled now. Why? Because the Gyspy staff grew tired of folks asking to take some dressing home in a to-go container! Now it's in bottles ready to be a much-loved souvenir. Give it a longer shelf life by making the bottle a vase after the dressing is gone.

19

CATCH THE PERFECT SUNSET

AT VILANO BEACH DINING HOT SPOTS

Cap's on the Water serves coastal cuisine and has a scenic dock, a covered pavilion, a tiki bar, a sunset oyster bar, and a beautiful deck covered in twinkly white lights with old oak trees growing right through it. It's a magical scene.

Aunt Kate's has been serving seafood for more than 100 years in a live oak grove on the bank of the Intracoastal. Enjoy sunset from the patio or the deck—another one that has old trees growing through it. At sunset, folks gather on the adjacent boat dock to watch nature put on a show.

Beaches at Vilano is where the locals go to feel like they're on vacation. It's like a piece of the Caribbean with the big deck, the big outdoor bar, and the big sunsets. Sit right in the sand and when the live music starts . . . don't worry, be happy.

Cap's on the Water
4325 Myrtle St., 904-824-8794
capsonthewater.com

Aunt Kate's
612 Euclid Ave., 904-829-1105
aunt-kates.com

Beaches at Vilano
254 Vilano Rd., Vilano Beach, 904-829-0589
beachesatvilano.com

FEAST ON A LIVE FIRE GRILLING CULINARY EXPERIENCE AT ASADOLIFE

With waterfront patio dining offering panoramic views of the San Sebastian River, AsadoLife hosts a live fire grilling experience. It's a true fire-and-water combination that enables guests to soak in the sights, sounds, and aromas of what's happening around them, making it the place to be. When AsadoLife opened, it was the talk of the town—and it still is.

Three experiences are available, and all must be booked in advance as the chef only prepares the amount of food that correlates with that day's reservations. Enjoy a four-course waterfront dinner, the Asador Club (which is a mix-and-mingle gathering with a private asador on the waterfront lounge), or the barcuterie with tapas and cocktails. There's nothing quite like the Asado experience, so yes, this is the place to post on Instagram to impress friends and enemies!

173 Shipyard Way, 904-501-1482
asadolife.com

21

PUT HAPPINESS IN A CUP
AT LOCAL COFFEE SHOPS

Cup 1: Serving locally brewed coffee, craft beer, wine, and house-baked treats, DOS hosts local musicians, writers, and artists. Part coffee shop, part local bar, DOS is pet friendly and sells coffee beans to go.

Cup 2: Offering fair-trade, organically grown coffee from Kenya, Ethiopia, Costa Rica, and Guatemala, Growers Alliance also showcases African crafts. Owners Martin and Purity grew up on coffee farms in Kenya and donate 10 percent of the coffee proceeds to the coffee farmers and their villages.

Cup 3: With six St. Augustine locations, the Kookaburra Coffee is a local favorite. An Aussie American espresso bar and pie shop, "the Kook" not only sells ethically sourced and roasted coffee, but also teaches brewing best practices via website videos.

Cup 4: Serving signature latte flavors such as hibiscus rose and lavender honey as well as all-day breakfast, Sweetwater Coffee Bar and Gallery has a gallery featuring work from resident artist Hannah Keats and owner, Sloane Keats.

DOS Coffee & Wine
300 San Marco Ave., 904-342-2421
dosbar.com

Growers Alliance
322 Anastasia Blvd.
growersalliance.com

The Kookaburra Coffee
Multiple locations
thekookaburracoffee.com

Sweetwater Coffee Bar and Gallery
8 Granada St., 904-615-1653
sweetwatercoffeebarandgallery.com

INDULGE IN A SOUTHERN BREAKFAST AT BLUE HEN CAFE

Head over to the Blue Hen Cafe on any day but Monday for an unforgettable breakfast, brunch, or lunch in a cozy dining room filled with southern hospitality. Serving locally sourced dishes from a scratch kitchen in the historic Lincolnville neighborhood, the Blue Hen is known for its southern specialties as well as its blue crab quiche and pumpkin pancakes (my favorites). Whether you're hankering for shrimp and grits, authentic southern biscuits, chipotle pimento cheese, or fried green tomatoes, the Blue Hen has it covered. It just may take a while, though, as everyone loves this joint, so the line is usually out the door. Once inside, be sure to enjoy all the vintage decorations—especially the hens, of course.

If you want lunch instead, try the fresh-catch tacos with a local beer. Whatever's on the plate, the old-school southern diner vibe is living large in this historic 1930s building with leather seating and checkered tablecloths. Don't forget to try something with the St. Augustine datil pepper—this makes for an überlocal dining experience.

117 M L King Ave., 904-217-3777
bluehencafe.com

TIP

While waiting for a table, take a stroll around Lincolnville, as there's no better way to admire the historic neighborhood than on two feet.

23

EMBRACE ST. AUGUSTINE'S ORIGINAL BEER PUB

AT RENDEZVOUS RESTAURANT

Don't even bother to look at Rendezvous Restaurant's menu—that's not why people come here. St. Augustine's original beer pub was established so all of us can enjoy the world-class beer selection. Born in 1986 before people could text about their favorite brews, the original beer pub doesn't look like much, but boy does it taste good. With more than 350 beer brands that change weekly, this family-run pub can quench thirsts with brews from Argentina to Zimbabwe. It's an around-the-world adventure that doesn't require a suitcase or a passport—only a deep love of good beer. Not sure what to drink? No worries. The bartenders can help, as they specialize in matching people with brews that make their taste buds happy.

St. George's Row, 106 St. George St., H, 904-824-1090

TIP

There's an entrance on Spanish Street and one in the St. George Row shopping mall on St. George Street.

DINE ALFRESCO
IN HISTORIC DOWNTOWN

Catch 27 prepares and serves fresh, locally caught seafood from Florida waters. It also serves the local specialty, Minorcan seafood chowder. The restaurant has many fans because of its local seafood, beautiful cocktails, historic downtown location, and delightful brick patio that's best enjoyed as the sun sets.

Harry's Seafood Bar & Grille serves southern, Cajun, and creole flavors in classic and modern dishes on a gorgeous brick patio across from the bay. The tree-lined patio is romantic, with little white twinkling lights and live music daily. They say if you haven't visited Harry's, you haven't visited St. Augustine.

River & Fort Restaurant & Rooftop Lounge offers a southern continental-inspired menu with second- and third-floor rooftops across the street from the Castillo de San Marcos. Having a cocktail against that backdrop makes for a perfect pit stop.

Catch 27
40 Charlotte St., 904-217-3542
catchtwentyseven.com

Harry's Seafood Bar & Grille
46 Avenida Menendez, 904-824-7765
hookedonharrys.com

River & Fort Restaurant & Rooftop Lounge
12 Avenida Menendez, 904-481-8396
riverandfort.com

25

LET'S TACO 'BOUT IT
AT THE TACO SHOPS AROUND TOWN

Make no mistake—St. Augustine is a city filled with tacos. Whether you have a craving at noon or midnight, there's a place to indulge in the city's favorite meal. My taco place of choice doesn't even have the word "taco" in the title. Back 40 Urban Café is an under-the-radar local favorite. Located just a block west of Route 1, Back 40 is in a charming old house and offers Taco Tuesday every day. Happy hour is from 2:30 to 5:30 p.m. daily, and the tacos are only $3 each. And let the record show that these are fabulous tacos, so be sure you arrive with an empty stomach. Choose from the taco menu, and you can enjoy a traditional taco or an avocado and roasted red pepper taco, a Key West tuna taco, or a Grouper taco. Bring a friend and order all eight types of tacos to share! It's a perfect way to get the taco lover off the beach before a sunburn sets in.

Back 40 Urban Café
40 S Dixie Hwy., 904-824-0227
back40cafe.com

Back 40 Urban Café
40 S Dixie Hwy., 904-824-0227
back40cafe.com

Burrito Works Taco Shop
114 St. George St., 904-823-1229
burritoworks.com

Gringos Tacos
125 King St., 904-217-0176
gringostacos.org

Mojo's Tacos
551 Anastasia Blvd., #4572, 904-829-1665

Osprey Tacos
300 Anastasia Blvd., 904-679-4191
ospreytacos.com

Taco Libre
1001 A1A Beach Blvd., 904-679-4230
tacolibrestaugustine.com

Tacos My Blessing
Food truck behind Bog Brewing
218 W King St., 904-829-4235
tacosmyblessingstaugustinefl.com

26

SAVE ROOM FOR DESSERT
AT THE AREA'S BEST BAKERIES

A scratch bakery owned and operated by local ladies, ChocoLattes features big, beautiful cakes and pastries, local Jacksonville coffee, as well as tea, wine, and beer.

Handcrafted desserts and hand-painted original flavor chocolates make Crème de la Cocoa heavenly. Stop in for a dessert shot—it will be the best $4 you ever spent.

Les Petits Pleasures, where Annecy, France, meets St. Augustine, Florida, offers a full array of French pastries as well as sweet and savory crepes—enjoy all without a passport.

Founded in 2008, LuLi's is St. Augustine's first cupcake shop and is especially popular with the locals. Their specialty cakes are fit for a cake museum should one ever pop up in town!

The gals who own Parfait Pastry Shop mix their Brazilian and Cuban roots with European influences in their pastry shop and café that rivals any in Spain, Portugal, or Italy.

ChocoLattes
47 Cordova St., 904-436-5813
chocolattes47.com

Crème de la Cocoa
299 San Marco Ave., 904-466-9499
cremedelacocoa.com

Les Petits Pleasures
125 A1A Beach Blvd., 904-679-3411

LuLi's Cupcakes & Bakery
82 San Marco Ave., 904-824-5280
luliscupcakes.com

Parfait Pastry Shop
142B King St., 904-217-3094
parfaitpastryshop.com

Dog Rose Brewing Co. hosts live music every weekend.

MUSIC AND ENTERTAINMENT

27

BE ODDLY ENTERTAINED
AT THE ODD MACABRE

The Odd Macabre claims to be "a great place to be yourself because . . . aren't we all a little odd?" Let your freak flag fly here—it's strongly encouraged! What is the Odd Macabre, anyway? It's a roving creative parlor that hosts ghost tours, paranormal investigations, scavenger hunts, true crime tours, witchcraft candle making, spooky shopping, and other devilish delights. For those who think Halloween should be celebrated all year, this is the place to be. Even for those who don't crave Halloween, remember . . . historic downtown is haunted, and this is the perfect place to be up close and personal with the undead. The Odd Macabre reminds us that the dark side is entertaining too.

904-217-9164
theoddmacabre.com

TIP

Visit the online parlor to see the adventures that are being offered during your visit. There will be many "weird and wonderfully mysterious things" to choose from that will take you to different haunted sites around town.

ODD MACABRE HIGHLIGHTS

The 13 Keys Scavenger and Mystery Hunt
A self-guided scavenger hunt filled with handcrafted games, clues, and of course, keys.

A Night Among Ghosts
Ghost tours and paranormal investigations revealing the Ancient City's histories, mysteries, and legends—some of whom are undead.

Truth . . . Stranger than Fiction Dark History Tour
History combines with the weird and wonderful on this Old City tour.

Madness and Malice True Crime Tour
A peek inside St. Augustine's dark side—historic crimes that led to murder.

28

EXPERIENCE LIVE MUSIC UTOPIA
AT THE AMP

The St. Augustine Amphitheatre, built in 1965 to commemorate St. Augustine's 400th anniversary, is the town's premier concert venue with just 4,900 seats. It hosts world-class performances and is lovingly called "the Amp" with a tagline that reads, "Big Acts, Small Venue," which is just one reason the community and the concert industry love the place. Another reason to fall in love with the Amp is the food trucks and the local craft beer and cocktails that make each event a tasty one. Yet another reason is the location on Anastasia Island, a half mile from the beach, surrounded by the natural landscape of Anastasia State Park. Camp there (or park for free in the lot) and jump on one of the free shuttles used to deliver concertgoers to the Amp. Hey big-city venues, beat that!

Utopia may not exist, but the Amp is sure close.

St. Augustine Amphitheatre
1340C A1A S, 904-209-3746
theamp.com

SWIM WITH THE DOLPHINS AT MARINELAND

The best scenic drive is along the A1A Scenic Byway from Ponte Vedra to Flagler Beach, and the best pit stop is just south of St. Augustine: Marineland Dolphin Adventure.

Marineland was the world's first oceanarium; however, it began as a movie studio. In 1938, "Marine Studios" opened and was the most popular tourist attraction in Florida. *Creature from the Black Lagoon* (1954) and *Benji Takes a Dive at Marineland* (1981) were filmed there.

The evolution from Marine Studios to Marineland started in the 1940s because of a diver's happy accident. He tried to distract hungry dolphins by throwing a fish into the water when one of them leapt up and caught it. The audience cheered in awe, as if this "trick" was planned, and soon after Marineland started hosting live dolphin shows.

Today, the emphasis is on connections to marine life, so humans can better understand and appreciate it.

Marineland Dolphin Adventure
9600 Oceanshore Blvd., 407-563-4701
marineland.net

30

ZIP OVER ALLIGATORS
AT THE ST. AUGUSTINE ALLIGATOR FARM

The St. Augustine Alligator Farm is an Old Florida staple, having been around since 1893. It's listed in the National Registry of Historic Places and is one of Florida's oldest continuously running attractions.

Over the years, the Alligator Farm has become a key proponent of wildlife research and conservation. The rookery—home to wild and unconfined herons, ibis, and egrets—operates in cooperation with the Florida Audubon Society. Since 1993, the Land of Crocodiles exhibit features all known species of the world's living crocodilians, making the Alligator Farm the only facility in the world exhibiting living examples of all 24 currently recognized species of crocodilian.

There's also zip-lining—right over the alligators! There's the Sepik River Course for beginners and the Nile River Course for intermediate zip liners. Both courses have daring souls flying through the park for 45–90 minutes, with feet dangling over alligators.

St. Augustine Alligator Farm Zoological Park
999 Anastasia Blvd., 904-824-3337
alligatorfarm.com

31

MIX AND MINGLE WITH LOCAL FELINES
AT THE CAT CAFÉS

Cat cafés have been all the rage in cities across Asia, Europe, and now in the United States. St. Augustine has two cat cafés! What are these feline-friendly cafés, anyway?

A cat café is a coffee shop where cat lovers can have a snack, enjoy a beverage, buy a souvenir—and pet cats! The cat lounge section of the café is full of happy, healthy, and relaxed cats available for adoption. Watch them play from the comfort of the café area or choose to pay a small fee to hang out in the lounge to mix and mingle with the kittens and cats. The "hang out" fee goes to feed, house, and care for the resident cats.

And the special events! There's Mewsic Nights with Kitties, Meowditation, Painting with Kitties, Mommy and Me Feline Jamboree, Yoga with Cats, and Happy Meower.

Frisky Cat Café
1092 S Ponce De Leon Blvd., 904-547-2940
friskycatcafe.com

The Witty Whisker Cat Cafe
112 N Ponce De Leon Blvd., Unit A, 904-342-5447
wittywhisker.com

32

SAIL AROUND TOWN
ON SCHOONER *FREEDOM* CHARTERS

There are several ways to see St. Augustine by water, but there's only one Schooner *Freedom*. The *Freedom* is the largest United States Coast Guard–certified sailing vessel in St. Augustine and is the only schooner charter vessel between Charleston and the Florida Keys. Built by naval architect Merritt Walters in 1982 in Norfolk, Virginia, the premier tall ship is 76 feet of steel and was brought to St. Augustine by the Zaruba family, who have logged thousands of sailing miles. With approximately 2,400 square feet of sail, the *Freedom* represents naval history and the privateers of the early 1800s. The Zaruba family is passionate about the ocean, sailing, and St. Augustine—guests can toast to all three when on the *Freedom*.

The *Freedom* was custom-built for use along the Intracoastal Waterway, making her the perfect vessel for the St. Augustine waters. Ahoy, matey!

111 Avenida Menendez, 904-810-1010
schoonerfreedom.com

33

EARN AN A+
ON A FLAGLER COLLEGE HISTORY TOUR

It's no secret that Flagler College used to be the luxurious Hotel Ponce de Leon. (Today's college is pretty luxurious, too.) Millionaire Henry Flagler built the hotel in 1888 and included all the bells and whistles of the time, including the largest collection of private Tiffany stained-glass windows in the world. With 79 stained-glass windows in the dining hall alone, the college is listed as a National Historic Landmark.

The public can tour the facilities to learn about its Spanish Renaissance architecture as well as those 79 Louis Comfort Tiffany stained-glass windows. The tour also showcases the 68-foot domed ceiling in the lobby and the handcrafted Austrian crystal chandeliers in the grand parlor. In Henry Flagler's time, the estate was worth a cool $100 million (more than $12.5 billion in today's dollars). If only we could all be Flagler College students for a day!

Flagler's Legacy, Historic Tours of Flagler College
59 St. George St., 904-823-3378
legacy.flagler.edu

TIP

Travel + Leisure named Flagler College one of the "25 Most Beautiful College Campuses in the United States."

CELEBRATE THE WINTER HOLIDAYS
AT THE NIGHTS OF LIGHTS

Did you know *National Geographic* named Nights of Lights as one of the "ten most dazzling holiday light displays in the world"? The annual winter holiday celebration begins the weekend before Thanksgiving and goes through the last day of January, showcasing millions of twinkling white lights on all the businesses in historic downtown.

While Nights of Lights has only been operational for 30 years, the event traces its origins back to the traditional Spanish practice of displaying a white candle in the window during the Christmas holidays. Since the Spanish founded St. Augustine more than 450 years ago, the city uses the white lights to connect to its history during the holiday season.

Some of the most elaborate lighting displays are at the Lightner Museum, Flagler College, the pedestrian-only St. George Street, Tini Martini and the Casablanca Inn, and the Bridge of Lions. The Plaza de la Constitución serves as the launching spot for the celebration, with the lights being turned on here first while a local band plays from the gazebo. Rumor has it that one red light is placed in one of the Plaza trees every year.

35

SPEND A SUNDAY FUNDAY
ON CRUISIN' TIKIS

If there's a tiki bar, it's a celebration. The floating ones in St. Augustine are even more special—not only do they float, but they're also motorized, so the bamboo, grass-roof huts offer a relaxing Sunday Funday (or any other day) on the water.

Pack some snacks, beverages, and up to five friends then join the captain and his Bluetooth sound system around the tiki bar. The captain has a freshwater sink and a cooler of ice waiting.

Wondering how much tiki to order? Do a 90-minute tour of the Matanzas Bay or add a beach excursion for a three-hour experience—or do a sunset cruise instead. Whatever the case, watch everyone on land be super jealous of the floating tiki celebration.

250 Vilano Rd., 904-980-8454
cruisintikisstaugustine.com

36

DANCE THE NIGHT AWAY
AT PROHIBITION KITCHEN

Everyone loves Prohibition Kitchen, so the line to get in is always long, and the music travels almost as far! The 1920s Prohibition era–themed gastropub hosts live music and serves locally sourced dishes and craft cocktails. The two-level seating area is done in a vintage industrial style—there are intimate booths with speakeasy vibes on the first floor and tables on the balcony level that overlook the stage and bar. When the building was renovated to create Prohibition Kitchen, reclaimed materials from the original colonial structure were used. Four-hundred-year-old heart of pine ceiling boards are now the bar and the booth tables. And the bar is the longest one in town—clearly this isn't a place to have a cup of tea!

119 St. George St., 904-209-5704
pkstaug.com

TIP

Wear dancing shoes; the seating fills up fast, so a lot of folks spend the entire evening on their feet.

37

GO ON A FRESHWATER SAFARI

WITH AIRBOAT ADVENTURES BY SEA SERPENT TOURS

Located at the much-beloved Trout Creek Fish Camp, Sea Serpent Tours hosts airboat rides on the St. Johns River and its tributaries. The locally-owned-and-operated tour operator explores the area's history and the natural environment west of St. Augustine on a six-passenger and a 15-passenger airboat. The father-daughter captain team has been featured in *Airboating Magazine*.

Considered a Freshwater Safari, the 90-minute airboat ride enables adventurers to see wildlife such as alligators, turtles, snakes, manatees, bald eagles, herons, and egrets—and, of course, the vegetation that provides homes and food for these local animals.

Want even more water? Sea Serpent Tours has other ways to get wet with kayaks, hydro-bikes, paddleboards, and pontoon boats. They also host tours on all of these "vessels" with sunset being prime time to enjoy the pontoon boats.

Trout Creek Marina Complex, 6550 SR-13 N, 904-495-4200
seaserpenttours.com

38

GET YOUR WILLY WONKA ON
AT WHETSTONE CHOCOLATES

Some towns offer chocolate tasting. St. Augustine offers tasting—and tours—of a chocolate shop born right here. Whetstone Chocolates began in 1967 as a small, family-run chocolate store. Now you can find them in several neighborhoods in St. Augustine, so when a sweet tooth needs attention, a shop is always close by.

Henry and Esther Whetstone first cornered the ice cream market, and then they set their minds to creating a chocolate brand—in their home kitchen at night after the ice cream shop closed. Whetstone Chocolates was born from that kitchen and is considered a great—and delicious—local success story.

Take a 45-minute tasting tour at the historic downtown Whetstone's and then "shop 'til you drop." Chocolate lovers from all over the world can be found enjoying the Whetstone chocolate, so be prepared to make new friends, too.

139 King St., 904-217-0275
whetstonechocolates.com

TIP

Want to bring chocolate home? The dark chocolate Menendez Shell Bag is a little bag of heaven—get two.

39

WALK THE PLANK
WITH BLACK RAVEN ADVENTURES

It has been said that St. Augustine used to be a fishing town with a drinking problem. It also used to be a drinking town with a pirate problem. Black Raven Adventures celebrates this heritage by hosting live, interactive pirate cruises. Designed and built to be a floating performance stage, the Black Raven's buccaneer crew of lads and lasses engages the audience as they present their unscripted pirate adventure. There are two ways to have this immersive pirate experience:

The all-ages Treasure Hunt stars Captain Hook and involves sword fights, cannon firings, a sea battle between the *Black Raven* and the *Queen Anne's Revenge*, treasure sharing, and sword-fighting lessons.

The 21-plus Rum Runners experience includes unscripted songs, comedy, scenes, stories, and of course lots of rum for sale at the cash bar—not for the easily offended!

111 Avenida Menendez, 904-826-0000
blackravenadventures.com

HOP AROUND TOWN
ON AN OLD TOWN TROLLEY TOUR

Like to get the lay of the land before taking a deep dive? Hop on the Old Town Trolley for a narrated tour of historic downtown with 22 stops along the way—the full loop takes approximately 80 minutes and covers 100 points of interest. It's the most comprehensive tour of St. Augustine, and riders can get on and off to eat, drink, shop, and sightsee. Other benefits include a breeze if it's hot, a ceiling if it's raining, and a rest no matter what the weather is doing!

A trolley ticket includes free parking at the Old Town Trolley Welcome Center, where discounted attraction packages are available for purchase. It also includes admission to the St. Augustine History Museum, shuttle service to many hotels, and Beach Bus service to the St. Augustine Alligator Farm and to St. Augustine Beach.

Plus, the trolley is a whole lotta fun to ride.

At the Old Jail, 167 San Marco Ave., 904-335-3155
trolleytours.com/st-augustine

41

EXPERIENCE HISTORY OR MAKE HISTORY
AT THE COLONIAL OAK

This two-acre attraction goes back in time—through three centuries—to showcase Colonial Spanish and British living history that made the nation's oldest city what it is today. Take an interactive, immersive tour with a Colonial Quarter resident, experience musket drills, climb to the top of a 17th-century watchtower replica, and then have an 18th century–style drink at the Bull and Crown or the Taberna del Caballo.

It's also home to Colonial Oak Music Park—an intimate venue filled with old live oaks and lanterns making for a nostalgic Old Florida atmosphere. Not only does "the Oak" feature nationally touring bands, but it also showcases local favorites including PAPERCUTT, the most highly sought-after cover band in town, playing '80s hair-band tunes. In 2023 the band celebrated its 20th anniversary—raising their glasses (and their hair) to fans and to the city of St. Augustine.

Colonial Quarter
14 S Castillo Dr., 904-342-2857
colonialquarter.com

Colonial Oak Music Park
27 St. George St., 904-342-2857
thecolonialoakmusicpark.com

HAVE AN INTIMATE ENCOUNTER
AT CAFE ELEVEN

An independent gem just a block off St. Augustine Beach, Cafe Eleven remains a local favorite for several reasons. They offer a great vegetarian menu, specialty coffee drinks, daily craft beer happy hours, and fabulous treats for the sweet tooth in all of us. Plus, there's an all-you-can-eat weekend brunch. And it's open seven days a week for all three meals.

And that's just the food and drink part of the business. It's also a well-loved and respected music venue for national touring bands. It's such a teeny-weeny spot that it doesn't even have a green room for artists. But boy does it have a stage. And when that stage is rocking, so are the folks who are lucky enough to have discovered the venue and the band on stage that night.

501 A1A Beach Blvd., 904-460-9311
originalcafe11.com

43

GET TO KNOW THE SPOOKY SIDE OF ST. AUGUSTINE

WITH A HAUNTED EXPERIENCE

St. Augustine is America's oldest city—and it's also America's most haunted city. While there are endless ways to mingle with the undead, there are a few that provide especially unique experiences.

The Old Jail After Dark: As seen on *Ghost Hunters* and *Kindred Spirits*, this epicenter of paranormal activity is in a historic building that housed prisoners between 1891 to 1953. The paranormal investigation, led by experts, may uncover strange phenomena using state-of-the-art equipment. Prepare to be surprised.

Dark of the Moon Ghost Tour at St. Augustine Lighthouse: The only tour that invites visitors onto the grounds after dark and includes a climb to the top of the lighthouse. Expect stories of ghostly encounters.

A Night Among Ghosts: Featured on the Travel Channel, this fully investigative experience combines history and hauntings. Each group of ghost hunters attempts to communicate with those "on the other side" via intuitive techniques, Victorian Spiritualism practices, and modern paranormal equipment. Not for nonbelievers.

Medieval Torture Museum: The first exclusively medieval torture museum in the country, the experience showcases torture devices, executions, and a ghost population. For strong stomachs only.

The Old Jail After Dark
167 San Marco Ave., 904-829-3800
trolleytours.com/st-augustine/old-jail-after-dark-tour

Dark of the Moon Ghost Tour at the Lighthouse
100 Red Cox Rd., 904-829-0745
staugustinelighthouse.org

A Night Among Ghosts
76 Spanish St., 904-217-9164
anightamongghosts.com

Medieval Torture Museum
100 St. George St., 904-373-7777
medievaltorturemuseum.com

44

TAKE A WALK DOWN MEMORY LANE

AT THE CLASSIC CAR MUSEUM OF ST. AUGUSTINE

The Classic Car Museum of St. Augustine showcases restored antique cars from the 1800s through the hot rods of the 1960s. Want to see a car from the "Greased Lightning" era? They got that. Want to see an Elvis-style Cadillac? They got that. Want to see something our great grandparents would have driven? They got that too! Classic trucks and service vehicles are also on display. Enjoy antique parts, gas pumps, and other period pieces as well as mini exhibits such as an old-time soda-fountain shop.

The 30,000-square-foot museum hosts monthly events such as Cars & Coffee and the Cruisers Car Club Cruise In. The place makes for a fabulous photo session, so consider wearing a vintage outfit and grabbing selfies with the cars of that era!

4730 Dixie Hwy.
ccmstaug.com

45

WHIZ AROUND TOWN

IN SOME FAR-OUT VEHICLES

Check out St. Augustine via golf cart, scooter, scoot coupe, or bike, or with a guided Segway tour. The aptly named Fun Rentals St. Augustine offers these nontraditional two- and four-wheeled options that make exploring historic downtown a breezy and even silly experience.

Drive down A1A in a brightly colored electric-powered Moke or a sleek two-passenger Polaris Slingshot courtesy of Seaside Adventures. The Moke, an emission-free vehicle, has a top speed of 25 miles per hour and is like an open-air fun ride for up to four people. The Polaris Slingshots, ground-hugging and sleek, are three-wheeled vehicles for two, and are just the thing to zip around town in while waving to everyone you leave behind.

All these untraditional vehicles provide great photo ops for Instagram and Facebook!

Fun Rentals St. Augustine
125 King St., Ste. A, 904-547-2074
funrentalsstaugustine.com

Seaside Adventures
606 N Ponce de Leon Blvd., 904-923-1010
seasideadventures.com

PLAY GAMES
IN THREE WAYS

Love some old-school '80s vibes? Head over to Anastasia Island's Arcade Museum for a craft soda, a jukebox tune, and a classic pinball or video game. Learn about arcade history while enjoying Pac-Man and friends.

Since 1978, Anastasia Miniature Golf has hosted an 18-hole mini golf course featuring a pirate ship, spooky tunnels, a tropical landscape, Japanese koi, numerous waterfalls, and golf tips—from pirates. The adventure is both fun and funny!

The three theme rooms at Escape U are Save the Fleet, the Sneaky Snake Lounge, and Old Jail. Each room combines storytelling, technology, and puzzle design to transport players to another place and time. Use investigative skills to find hidden clues, decipher codes, and unlock the room in less than an hour's time.

Anastasia Island's Arcade Museum
2085 A1A S, Unit 206

Anastasia Miniature Golf
701 Anastasia Blvd., 904-825-0101
anastasiaminigolf.com

Escape U
525 FL-16, Unit 104, 904-687-0022
escapeuflorida.com

CRUISE THE WATERWAYS

ON ST. AUGUSTINE SCENIC CRUISE

For more than 100 years, St. Augustine Scenic Cruise has been giving visitors a unique view of the city. Run by the Usina family, one of the original Minorcan families to settle in St. Augustine, the Scenic Cruise started when Frank Usina and his wife ferried Henry Flagler's guests to North Beach for Minorcan-style dinners. Shortly after these excursions from the Ponce de Leon Hotel began, the Usinas purchased a 45-foot boat that was stuck in a mud bar. They repaired and refinished it, naming the vessel the *Victory*. In 1918, Frank Usina's son helped launch *Victory II*, which was the only mode of transportation to North Beach from historic downtown until the '30s, when a paved highway and bridge were built for cars.

In 1949, *Victory II* became a full-time sightseeing boat. Since then, its riders have been taking a deep dive into history—pun intended!

111 Avenida Menedez, 904-824-1806
scenic-cruise.com

48

HAVE AN ADVENTURE
IN THE LIMELIGHT

Established in 1992, Limelight Theatre is the only year-round community theater in town. It offers eight mainstage productions each season, as well as theater education for both kids and grown-ups. To say there's always a lot going on "in the Limelight" is an understatement. Check out what's playing and enjoy dinner before the show at neighboring Raintree Restaurant—perfect for a date night.

Now imagine opening a piece of candy to find a treat in the center—that's the Adventure Project. Housed in Limelight Theatre, the Adventure Project is St. Augustine's home for improvisational theater. With a five-level improv training school for grown-ups, kids' camps, and unscripted shows and theater experiences, the Adventure Project keeps locals and visitors laughing—no script needed. (The shows are based on audience suggestions, so be prepared to participate!)

Want another performance adventure?

Just up the road is the St. Augustine Waterworks, which is on the National Register of Historic Places. Built in 1898 as the city waterworks, it later became a community center and theater and then closed in 2005. The city restored the historic building, and St. Johns Cultural Council reopened it in 2022 to host cultural and heritage events including theater, dance, opera, poetry, and music performances.

Limelight Theatre
11 Old Mission Ave., 904-825-1164
limelight-theatre.org

Raintree Restaurant
102 San Marco Ave., 904-824-7211
raintreerestaurant.com

The Adventure Project
adventure-project.com

St. Augustine Waterworks
184 San Marco Ave., 904-808-7330
stjohnsculture.com/the-waterworks

Washington Oaks Gardens State Park makes for a picture-perfect picnic spot.

SPORTS AND RECREATION

HAVE AN AWARD-WINNING NATURAL EXPERIENCE

AT ANASTASIA STATE PARK

Anastasia State Park ranks sixth on the list of best state parks in the United States and is known for bicycling, camping, windsurfing, kayaking, fishing, hiking, swimming, and sailing. With 1,600 acres of dunes and tidal marshes as well as four miles of white quartz sand beaches, it offers explorers a chance to see osprey, warblers, spoonbills, buntings, eagles, and other wildlife, especially when walking the Ancient Dunes Nature Trail.

Anastasia State Park backs up to the St. Augustine Amphitheatre, so campers can stay in one of the 139 campsites when seeing a show. *Travel + Leisure* magazine has included the park on its list of prettiest beach campsites.

The park is connected to the town's history as well. An archaeological site, Coquina Quarry, is inside the park—this is where coquina rock was mined to build the Castillo de San Marcos National Monument.

300 Anastasia Park Rd., 904-461-2033
floridastateparks.org/anastasia

SOAK IN THE PERFECT RIVERSIDE SUNSET

AT ALPINE GROVES PARK

Don't be fooled by the term "alpine" or the "Switzerland" address—there is no place more representative of Old Florida than Alpine Groves Park in Switzerland, which is 30 miles northeast of historic downtown. With panoramic views of the St. Johns River, the park is the perfect place to take in a sunset (just bring bug spray). Plus, the drive to and from is gorgeous, as State Road 13 hugs the river and is filled with old oak trees. Hike in the park and enjoy butterfly gardens, historical homes, horse stables, and wildlife such as tortoises, owls, manatees, and alligators. The Garden Club of Switzerland maintains the park which, has a history intertwined with the booming citrus industry of the 19th century. Because it was once an orange grove homestead, there are a variety of citrus trees, and an orange-grove-themed playground connecting the past to the present.

2060 SR 13, Switzerland, 904-209-0333
co.st-johns.fl.us/recreation/parks/alpinegroves.aspx

STOP AND SMELL THE ROSES AT WASHINGTON OAKS GARDENS STATE PARK

Just south of St. Augustine, along the A1A Scenic and Historic Coastal Byway, lies Washington Oaks Gardens State Park—on both sides of the road. On the east side is a unique shoreline with rare coquina rock outcroppings, which makes for some interesting photos. And on the west side are formal gardens with old oak trees, nature trails, reflection ponds, and the Intracoastal Waterway. Here you can hike, bike, picnic, and soak in the rose garden, which is a picture-perfect spot to take Instagram-worthy shots. With an average of 150 rose bushes blooming, this is the largest public rose garden on the Florida coast. Want to see it in all its splendor? Visit at the beginning of May.

Washington Oaks also hosts special events throughout the year. Most visitors discover that stopping to smell the roses is special enough.

6400 N Oceanshore Blvd., Palm Coast, 386-446-6780
floridastateparks.org/parks-and-trails/washington-oaks-gardens-state-park

52

EXPLORE PROTECTED NATURE

AT GUANA TOLOMATO MATANZAS NATIONAL ESTUARINE RESEARCH RESERVE

The Guana Tolomato Matanzas National Estuarine Research Reserve (GTMNERR) protects 76,000 acres of Florida's northeast coastline, from Ponte Vedra Beach to Palm Coast. St. Augustine is smack dab in the middle.

The northern end has the Tolomato and Guana River estuaries and features more than 10 miles of trails through a variety of protected habitats, as well as scenic boardwalks along A1A that offer three beach access points. There are hiking, biking, horseback riding, fishing, kayaking, beachcombing, a visitor center, and a scary forest on Halloween weekend.

The southern end has the Matanzas River and several state parks, including Pellicer Creek Aquatic Preserve, Faver-Dykes State Park, Washington Oaks Gardens State Park, and the River to Sea Preserve at Marineland.

The GTM Research Reserve is one of only 28 national estuarine research reserves in the country, all focused on research, public education, and protecting the natural biodiversity in the estuary.

505 Guana River Rd., Ponte Vedra Beach, 904-380-8600
gtmnerr.org

53

DEVELOP A PEACEFUL RELATIONSHIP

WITH NATURE AT BELUTHAHATCHEE PARK WITH EARTH KINSHIP

Designed by Florida Hall of Fame inductee, journalist, and author Stetson Kennedy, Beluthahatchee Park is a peaceful haven that connects people with nature. Large oak trees protect the natural habitat where herons, egrets, eagles, ducks, and other species live. Learn about the different types of vegetation while exploring scenic trails and the Stetson Kennedy residence. Get more insight into the history of the park and its mission, culture, and wildlife conservation efforts at the main house.

Earth Kinship, a locally-owned-and-operated ecotourism company, helps to create bonds between people and the natural environment. Hosting kayak tours, camping trips, forest therapy, arts events, history programs, and guided hikes, Earth Kinship invites participants to become friends with nature by showcasing the natural world just outside St. Augustine. Owner Ayolane Halusky has more than 20 years of experience in the natural world and serves as the lead steward. Offering a deep dive into nature, Earth Kinship has been known to turn visitors into naturalists.

Beluthahatchee Park
1523 SR 13, Fruit Cove
sjcfl.us/lamp/projects/flct_belutha.aspx

Earth Kinship
5880 Don Manuel Rd., Elkton
904-477-5669, earthkinship.us

HAVE A SCENIC TWO-WHEELED ADVENTURE

ON THE PALATKA TO ST. AUGUSTINE STATE TRAIL

Love to explore on two wheels? Check out the Palatka to St. Augustine State Trail which travels through rural communities including Elkton, Armstrong, Hastings, and East Palatka. This 19-mile paved trail runs through agricultural and scenic landscapes linking the designated Florida Trail Town, Palatka, to St. Augustine. Starting in St. Augustine and going west to Palatka, discover kiosks with trail maps, restrooms, picnic areas, and playgrounds as well as five different trailheads.

The Palatka to St. Augustine State Trail is also a part of the St. Johns River to Sea Loop. This 260-mile multiuse trail is the longest loop trail through the American Southeast. The loop links a national seashore, Florida state parks, monuments, wildlife refuges, springs, and museums.

386-329-3721
floridastateparks.org/parks-and-trails/palatka-st-augustine-state-trail

55

ENJOY A QUIETER, SIMPLER TIME

AT GENUNG'S FISH CAMP

In 1948, Jack Genung founded Genung's Fish Camp on the Matanzas River. He ran the classic Florida bait shop for almost 50 years, making it into a community gathering spot for fishermen, surfers, and the local kids. Today, the Morley family runs the camp and keeps true to its local roots. First and foremost a bait-and-tackle shop, Genung's carries inshore saltwater tackle, live shrimp, and mud minnows, as well as frozen and artificial bait. The shop also carries cold drinks, local beer, hats, sunscreen, and T-shirts, as well as snacks and eco-friendly products.

With a small marina, Genung's has boat slip rentals, a mechanic, and guided fishing excursions, as well as kayak, canoe, and stand-up paddleboard rentals. Genung's also hosts special events such as pizza nights, oyster roasts, and local artist evenings.

GeoTrippin' Adventure Co. is there as well, offering kayak tours with a focus on the environment and local history.

Genung's also houses the Matanzas Riverkeeper, which runs the Litter Gitter program, taking visitors and locals out on the water to remove trash and to learn about marine debris and litter issues. The namesake, the *Litter Gitter II*, a 24-foot Carolina skiff, is specially equipped to remove debris from the local waterways. Volunteers can get their hands dirty while also taking a fabulous ride down the Matanzas. Win-win!

Genung's Fish Camp
291 Cubbedge Rd., 904-907-5742
genungsfishcamp.com

GeoTrippin' Adventure Co.
291 Cubbedge Rd., 904-701-3272
geotrippin.com

Matanzas Riverkeeper
291 Cubbedge Rd., 904-471-9878
matanzasriverkeeper.org

COME SAIL AWAY
WITH ST. AUGUSTINE SAILING

Want to learn how to sail? St. Augustine Sailing has you covered. There are few things the crew enjoys more than turning landlubbers into sailors. St. Augustine Sailing offers several charters that introduce newbies to sailing. Some are fully hands-on, while others offer relaxation in affordable luxury.

St. Augustine Sailing has two ways to learn sailing:

The first is Intro to Sailing, which gives two to four people a chance to learn sailing basics including sail handling and steering as well as finding that elusive wind.

The next is Learn the Ropes, which gives more experienced sailors access to a bigger boat and more detailed instruction.

3076 Harbor Dr., 904-829-0648
sta-sail.com

57

CATCH A FISH OR A SUNSET
AT MATANZAS INLET

The Matanzas Inlet is unique in several ways. From a historical perspective, the inlet had an interesting role as the spot where the Spanish, led by Pedro Menéndez de Avilés, massacred French forces in 1565, helping to secure Spanish control of Florida for 235 years.

From a natural angle, the park has 300 acres and four different ecosystems: the Atlantic Ocean with the beach sand, dunes, and dune meadows; the coastal scrub; the maritime forest; and the Matanzas River estuary. It's also a great spot to take a dip on a hot day.

And in terms of pure fun, the inlet hosts a food boat—the Salty Beach Snak Shak "parks" in the Matanzas on weekends keeping fisher-people, swimmers, kayakers, and sunbathers fed via tacos, quesadillas, empanadas, hot dogs, cookies, ice cream, and frozen treats.

About 15 miles south of historic downtown on Highway A1A

TIP

You can see one of the most beautiful sunsets in St. Augustine from the Matanzas Inlet.

TAKE A WALK OVER TROUBLED WATERS VIA THE VILANO BRIDGE AND THE BRIDGE OF LIONS

Take a walk over the Vilano Bridge or the Bridge of Lions for different perspectives of the city. Think about the water below and how it was once a battleground for pirates and wannabe conquerors trying to steal the town from the Spanish. The two bridges are 1.2 miles apart and make for a great sunrise run. The Bridge of Lions is a hop and a skip from one side to the other, while the Vilano Bridge is 1.5 miles long, making it a windy, wonderful experience whether you're crossing it at sunrise or sunset.

The Vilano Bridge is also connected to the Vilano Beach Nature Boardwalk, which not everyone realizes. The quarter-mile boardwalk goes under the bridge and offers scenic salt marsh views as well as wildlife mosaics. The boardwalk connects the residential neighborhood with the Vilano Beach Town Center, with parking available on both sides.

Vilano Bridge
Connects St. Augustine to Vilano Beach

Bridge of Lions
Connects historic downtown to Anastasia Island

Built in 1927, the Bridge of Lions was added to the National Register of Historic Places in 1982. The two lions, Firm and Faithful, guard the bridge and are made from marble that originated in the same quarry as the stone used in Michelangelo's David.

EMBRACE BEACH LIFE ON A STREET WITH A PIT STOP

AT THE BEACHCOMBER

A Street is where all good things begin on St. Augustine Beach. Have a smoothie, a taco, or a beer. Lie in a hammock, sit on a deck, or lounge seaside. Use this as an access point to walk, bike, or park on the beach. And of course, don't forget the sunblock and surfboard for catching some rays in between catching some waves. It's one glorious block of beach life that's worthy of rinsing and repeating over and over.

Take a break from sunbathing, surfing, and swimming at the Beachcomber restaurant—"where A Street meets the ocean." Sit on the deck or put your feet in the sand to lounge while enjoying chowders, street tacos, seafood, local beer, or tropical island cocktails. The kids—and the dogs—love the Beachcomber too, as there's a sand pit play area with beach toys that sits at the bottom of the A Street sand dune.

Bring home an A Street souvenir with a Beachcomber koozie or T-shirt.

2 A St., St. Augustine Beach, 904-471-3744
beachcomberstaugustine.com

FOR THE FULL A STREET EXPERIENCE . . .

Burrito Works Taco Shop
671 A1A Beach Blvd., St. Augustine Beach, 904-217-7451
burritoworks.com

Jacks Bar-B-Que and Bootlegger Beach Brewing
691 A1A Beach Blvd., St. Augustine Beach, 904-460-8100

Pit Surf Shop
18 A St., St. Augustine Beach, 904-471-4700
pitsurfshop.com

Stir it Up
18 A St., St. Augustine Beach, 904-461-4552
stiritupstaug.com

Mango Mango's
700 A1A Beach Blvd., St. Augustine Beach, 904-461-1077
mangomangos.com

60

FLY HIGH OVER THE WATER
VIA ST. AUGUSTINE PARASAIL AND FIRST CITY HELICOPTERS

After experiencing St. Augustine on the water, it seems only right to experience it over the water. How? Via St. Augustine Parasail. Parasail tours are available at 500 or 1,000 feet above the city's waterways. Snag a photo package for proof that the St. Augustine flying adventure really happened!

The other option is via a bright yellow helicopter named Bee, courtesy of First City Helicopters. Lifting off from the Northeast Florida Regional Airport in St. Augustine, the bird's-eye tours run between eight and 40 miles. From North Beach to Vilano Beach to the St. Augustine Lighthouse to Fort Matanzas to historic downtown, Bee offers visitors a perspective like no other. With three packages to choose from, you can select the amount of airtime that's suitable for the budget—and for the stomach!

St. Augustine Parasail
111-C Avenida Menendez, 904-547-9608
staugustineparasail.com

First City Helicopters
4900 US Hwy. 1 N, Ste. 400, 904-824-5506
firstcityhelicopters.com

61

WATCH THE SUN COME UP

AT THE BEACH OR IN TOWN

With 42 miles of beaches, St. Augustine has several picture-perfect places to see the sun come up. The northern (North Beach) and southern beaches (Crescent Beach, Matanzas Beach) have wonderful views and "treasure hunting" opportunities once the sun is up. Keep an eye out for sea glass and shark teeth, as well as unique shells and rocks.

In town, watch the sun rise over the bay from the Castillo de San Marcos at the north end of the seawall or head to the south end and grab a spot at the National Guard headquarters, St. Francis Barracks. In the historic Lincolnville neighborhood, you can see the sun rise over the Matanzas at Dr. Robert B. Hayling Freedom Park through the Freedom Chimes.

North Beach Park
3721 Coastal Hwy.

Crescent Beach Park
6930 A1A S, Crescent Beach

Matanzas Beach and Inlet
8655 A1A S

Castillo de San Marcos
National Monument
11 S Castillo Dr.

St. Francis Barracks
82 Marine St.

Dr. Robert B. Hayling Freedom Park
601 Riberia St.

TIP

Heading to North Beach? Check out all the "locks of love" attached to the North Beach Park beach access bridge.

The Castillo de San Marcos is the oldest masonry fort in the continental United States.

CULTURE AND HISTORY

TAKE A DRINK
FROM THE FOUNTAIN OF YOUTH

A 15-acre waterfront historical attraction, the Fountain of Youth Archaeological Park, tells the story of the first Spanish settlers who came to St. Augustine in the 1600s and the native Timucuans who were here to greet them. The park has a working archaeological dig on-site, as well as several re-created Spanish and Timucuan buildings. It also hosts a variety of shows and living history reenactments for edutainment.

The best part of the Fountain of Youth is the water, of course. Drink from the natural spring that is said to have special properties that will restore a youthful glow. The other best part of the visit is the free-roaming peacocks that often leave the property and wander the neighboring streets and yards "talking" to each other as they strut around the area.

11 Magnolia Ave., 904-829-3168
fountainofyouthflorida.com

TIP

Enjoy the views from the 600-foot Founders Riverwalk and from the observation tower, too.

LIGHT UP THE NIGHT
AT THE ST. AUGUSTINE LIGHTHOUSE & MARITIME MUSEUM

Standing 165 feet above sea level, overlooking the Matanzas Bay and the Atlantic Ocean from Anastasia Island, the St. Augustine Lighthouse serves as a scenic and educational maritime museum. Climb the 219 steps to the top for a well-earned view of the city and the Atlantic Ocean. Along the way discover fun facts and stories about the lighthouse, including the one about Smokey the Lighthouse Cat, who lived with the lighthouse keepers during the Great Depression.

Besides the lighthouse, the Keeper's House Museum, the marine archeologists' work, and boat-building demonstrations, there's also the guided paranormal Dark of the Moon Ghost Tour. Learn the ghostly history of the grounds, climb the lighthouse stair in the dark, and conduct a paranormal investigation. *USA Today* named the St. Augustine Lighthouse as one of the 10 best haunted locations in the United States. It's also been featured on A&E's *Ghost Hunters* show.

100 Red Cox Rd., 904-829-0745
staugustinelighthouse.org

64

DISCOVER A PARANORMAL PARADISE
AT THE OLD JAIL

Home to prisoners for more than 60 years from 1891 to 1953, the Old Jail is listed on the National Register of Historic Places. Henry Flagler (remember him?) built the jail to look like a hotel in the Romanesque Revival style, so it resembles a resort rather than a maximum-security prison. During the day you can learn about the prisoners and practices as well as the sheriffs who ran the place. At night, discover a "paranormal paradise" with the Old Jail After Dark experience as seen on *Ghost Hunters* and *Kindred Spirits*. Use ghost-hunting equipment to connect to the other side with an intimate group of ghost hunters led by an expert guide in what's considered one of the most haunted buildings in the country. Afterward, discuss the group's findings while the ghost-hunting expert helps rule out any logical reasons for the discoveries.

167 San Marco Ave., 904-829-3800
trolleytours.com/st-augustine/old-jail

ENJOY EVENTS
AT THE PLAZA DE LA CONSTITUCIÓN

When someone says, "The Plaza," they are referring to the Plaza de la Constitución, which sits in historic downtown on the west side of the Bridge of Lions. Featuring a central pavilion and a public market that's been around since the 1500s, it's also where the Nights of Lights celebration kicks off each year. It's home to several remembrances, including the obelisk celebrating the Spanish Constitution of 1812 as well as statues honoring American Revolution prisoners; one to honor soldiers killed in World War II, the Korean War, and the Vietnam War; and an installation commemorating St. Augustine's role in the Civil Rights Movement. The latter is known as the Foot Soldiers Monument.

The Plaza is also a beautiful place to take in the city from a park bench with a sweet tea or a lemonade. It makes for a great rest stop during the First Friday Artwalk. And it's a perfect meeting spot if your fellow travelers want to split up for a bit.

1 Cathedral St., 904-825-1001

TIP

Enjoy events at the Plaza such as the summer Concerts in the Plaza series and the winter Nights of Lights display. The Plaza is surrounded by large cannon statues, which make for fun photos with (or without) kids.

66

HONOR THE AFRICAN AMERICAN EXPERIENCE

AT THE ACCORD CIVIL RIGHTS MUSEUM AND FREEDOM TRAIL

Historic Lincolnville dates back more than 450 years and is the epicenter of the African American experience, playing a significant role in the Civil Rights Movement of the 1960s.

The ACCORD (Anniversary to Commemorate the Civil Rights Demonstrations) Civil Rights Museum recognizes the "local heroes and sheroes" of St. Augustine's Civil Rights Movement. The museum, located on a residential street in Lincolnville, was once Dr. Robert B. Hayling's dental office—he is known as the "Father of St. Augustine's civil rights."

The ACCORD Freedom Trail guides walkers through 31 historic sites with markers to read along the way. The trail's mission is "remembering, recognizing, and honoring all those who risked their lives to attain civil rights for all and celebrating St. Augustine's pivotal role in the Civil Rights Act of 1964."

79 Bridge St., 904-347-1382
accordfreedomtrail.org/ACCORDCivilRightsMuseum.html
(call for an appointment)
accordfreedomtrail.org/sites.html (for a list of places on the walking tour)

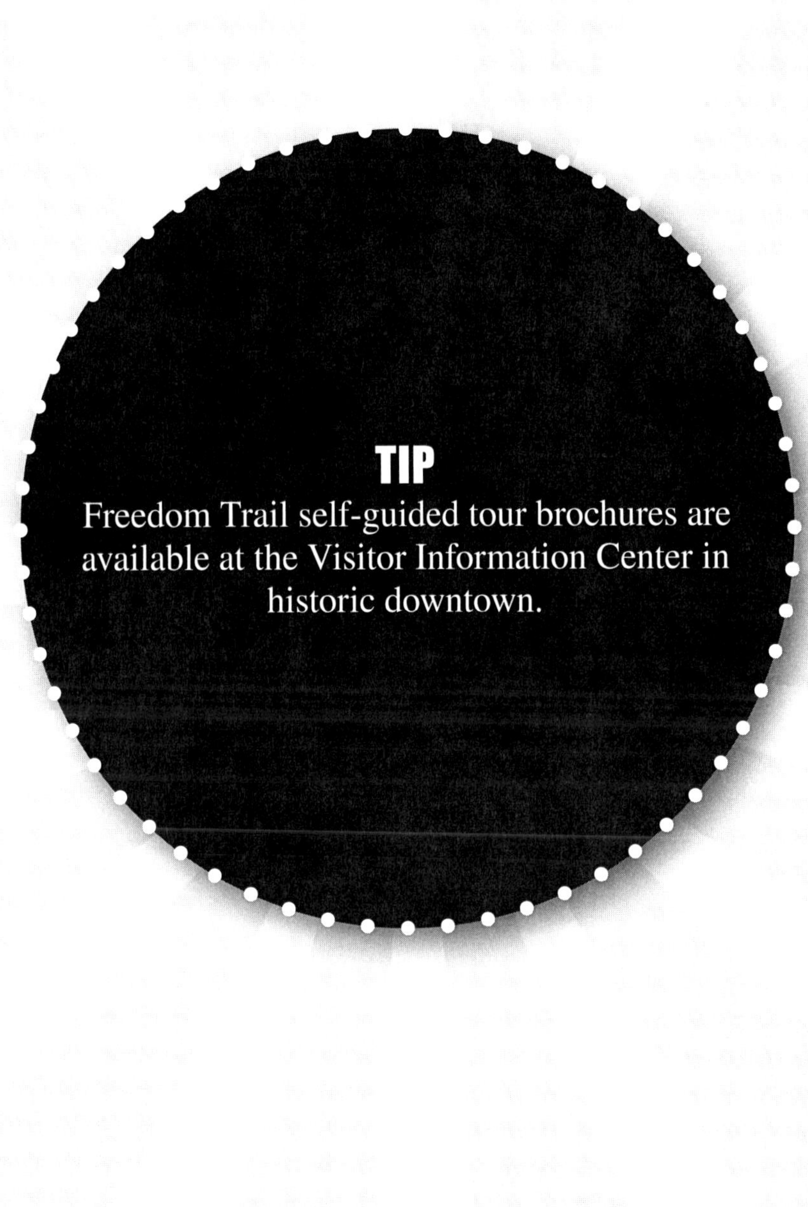
TIP
Freedom Trail self-guided tour brochures are available at the Visitor Information Center in historic downtown.

VISIT THIS OLD HOUSE
IN HISTORIC DOWNTOWN ST. AUGUSTINE

An original American treasure, the Oldest Wooden School House Historic Museum & Gardens showcases a Minorcan homestead and school life from the 1800s. View copies of old textbooks and school supplies, and then tour the kitchen and gardens where a pecan tree has been growing for an estimated 250 years. (Notice the house has a large chain wrapped around it to hold it in place in case of hurricane-force winds.)

The St. Augustine Historical Society runs the Oldest House Museum Complex and offers a guided tour of Florida's oldest house, two museums, ornamental gardens, a colonial kitchen, and the museum shop. Also known as the Gonzalez-Alvarez House, it's the oldest surviving Spanish colonial residence in Florida.

Built during the First Spanish Period, the Father Miguel O'Reilly House Museum is one of the oldest structures in town, in the oldest continuously settled neighborhood. Constructed in 1691 of tabby and coquina, the building was purchased by Father Miguel O'Reilly in 1785. An Irish priest serving the Spanish crown, he made the house a place for spirituality and education.

TIP

The complex houses the St. Augustine Surf Culture and History Museum, an interactive museum that interprets oral histories and historical images as well as containing film, music, artifacts, memorabilia, trophies, articles, and historic surfboards.

Oldest Wooden School House Historic Museum & Gardens
14 St. George St., 904-824-0192
oldestwoodenschoolhouse.com

Oldest House Museum Complex
14 St. Francis St., 904-824-2872
staughs.com/oldest-house-museum-complex

Father Miguel O'Reilly House Museum
32 Aviles St., 904-826-0750
fatheroreilly.house

68

VISIT HISTORIC HOUSES OF WORSHIP IN DOWNTOWN ST. AUGUSTINE

Downtown St. Augustine is home to several historic religious sites representing a variety of denominations that reflect its early settlers. Houses of worship such as the Methodist church, the Greek Orthodox shrine, and the Catholic cathedral basilica offer a glimpse of early settler living and worship. By establishing these religious sites, the various denominations found a home in the New World while adding to St. Augustine's rich—and diverse—history.

While most of these historic religious sites are based in Christianity, the First Congregation Sons of Israel was founded in 1908 when Eastern European Jews settled in St. Augustine. The synagogue was built in 1923, with the first service held in 1924. Since then, the congregation added a social hall and a small school.

Since the turn of the century, the historic building—like many others downtown—was damaged by hurricanes. A local cushion maker restored the old theater seats. A local craftsman restored the wooden seats. The original floors were saved, too. However, the ceiling decoration was lost—it's since been replaced by a period-appropriate Star of David that a Flagler student created and designed.

First Congregation Sons of Israel
161 Cordova St., 904-829-9532
firstcongregationsonsofisrael.com

Ancient City Baptist Church
27 Sevilla St., 904-829-3476, ancientcitybaptist.org

Cathedral Basilica of St. Augustine
38 Cathedral Pl., 904-824-2806
dosafl.com/parish/cathedral-basilica-of-st-augustine

Grace United Methodist Church
8 Carrera St., 904-829-8272, gracestaugustine.org

Memorial Presbyterian Church
32 Sevilla St., 904-829-6451, memorialpcusa.org

St. Benedict the Moor Mission
86 Martin Luther King Ave., 904-824-2806
dosafl.com/parish/st-benedict-the-moor-mission

St. Cyprian's Episcopal Church
37 Lovett St., 904-829-8828, stcypriansepiscopalchurch.org

St. Paul AME Church
85 Martin Luther King Ave., 904-829-3918, saintpaulfamily.com

St. Photios Greek Orthodox National Shrine
41 St. George St., 904-829-8205, stphotios.org

National Shrine of Our Lady of La Leche at Mission Nombre de Dios
101 San Marco Ave., (904) 824-2809, missionandshrine.org

Trinity Parish Episcopal Church
215 St. George St., 904-824-2876, trinitysta.org

LEARN ABOUT BLACK HERITAGE
AT THE LINCOLNVILLE MUSEUM AND CULTURAL CENTER

The Lincolnville Museum and Cultural Center is housed in the building that opened as St. Augustine's first Black public high school in 1902. The museum examines history through the city's Black population, from its first Black resident—Juan Garrido—to today's history makers. (Juan Garrido arrived with Juan Ponce de Leon—the first European in St. Augustine—in 1513.)

The museum's exhibits showcase Black music, businesses, military service, and history—especially as they related to St. Augustine's role in the Civil Rights Movement. In the 1960s, St. Augustine was a violent, segregated city and the site of protests to combat racism. One protest, in July 1963, got Dr. Martin Luther King Jr.'s attention. Four Black teenagers went to the local Woolworths and sat at the "whites-only" counter to eat hamburgers and to enjoy each other's company. Although they were minors, the police took them to jail, placing them in an adult facility. The museum houses an exhibit that recognizes "the St. Augustine Four." Included in the exhibit is a section of the original Woolworth's counter as well as Dr. King's fingerprint card from his 1964 St. Augustine arrest.

102 MLK Ave., 904-824-1191
lincolnvillemuseum.org

FEEL FANCY AND FINE
AT THE LIGHTNER MUSEUM

In the building that was once the Hotel Alcazar, a Gilded Age resort hotel that railroad magnate Henry Flagler built in 1888, the Lightner Museum offers an experience that's part art, part architecture, part history, part design, and all gorgeous.

Founded by Chicago publisher Otto Lightner in 1948, the museum showcases his unique collection of Americana, fine and decorative art, Tiffany lamps, American and European paintings, and Victorian mechanical musical instruments, as well as geological specimens and shells collected from all over the world.

When it was the Alcazar Hotel, the Spanish Renaissance Revival building hosted guests who enjoyed recreation facilities including the world's largest swimming pool, Turkish and Russian steam baths, tennis courts, and a gymnasium. The Alcazar closed during the Depression and was transformed into Lightner's eclectic museum.

75 King St., 904-824-2874
lightnermuseum.org

TIP

Don't miss the koi fishpond surrounded by tropical plants and palm trees in the center of the courtyard.

REENACT HISTORY
AT ST. AUGUSTINE'S FORTS

St. Augustine's crown jewel, the Castillo de San Marcos, is the oldest masonry fort in the continental United States at more than 300 years old. This national monument and Spanish stone fortress was built to protect Spain's turf in the New World. Check out the rooms that once housed soldiers and prisoners, visit the interior courtyard and gun deck with spectacular city views, and observe actual cannon firings and weaponry demonstrations from historians and reenactors in period clothing.

Fort Matanzas has been standing in the Matanzas Inlet for more than 250 years after defending the city from British attack. Ride the free ferry from the visitor center to the other side of the inlet, and then enjoy history as well as a boardwalk trail through the maritime forest.

Although the actual Fort Mose is no longer standing, its memory remains, as it was the site of the first legally sanctioned free African American settlement. Recognized as a National Historic Landmark in 1994, Fort Mose is also a precursor site of the National Underground Railroad Network as it was built specifically for Blacks fleeing slavery in the English colonies.

FUN FACT

The word "matanzas" in Spanish translates to "slaughters" in English.

Castillo de San Marcos National Monument
1 S Castillo Dr., 904-829-6506
nps.gov/casa/index.htm

Fort Matanzas National Monument
8635 A1A S, 904-471-0116
nps.gov/foma/index.htm

Fort Mose Historic State Park
15 Fort Mose Trail, 904-823-2232
floridastateparks.org/parks-and-trails/fort-mose-historic-state-park

72

SEE THE DOCTOR
AT THE SPANISH MILITARY HOSPITAL MUSEUM

Travel back in time at the Spanish Military Hospital Museum to learn about medical practices and procedures from St. Augustine's Spanish colonial period. The guided tour showcases colonial surgery techniques via demonstrations with "doctors" (museum guides) and "patients" (visitors) that show how antique surgical instruments were used. Afterward, you can visit the museum's surgical instrument collection.

The museum apothecary reveals how the period's herbs were the origins of some of the most common modern medicines. Many of these herbs can be found on-site in the apothecary's garden.

The Spanish Military Hospital Museum is an authentic reconstruction of a military hospital that once stood on this site. The museum explains how Spanish physicians combined medical information from Europe and Africa to achieve an astonishing survival rate, putting Spanish medicine some 400 years ahead of practices in other European nations.

The attraction is pet friendly too.

3 Aviles St., 904-342-7730
smhmuseum.com

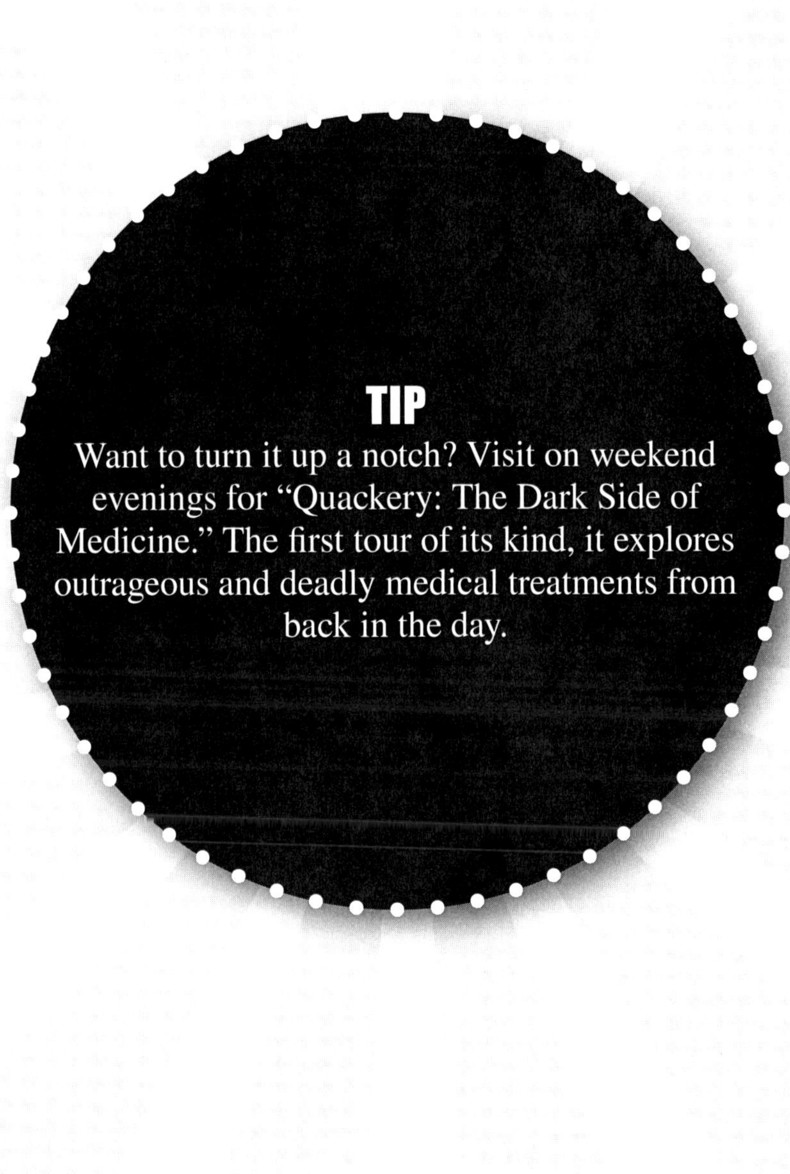

TIP

Want to turn it up a notch? Visit on weekend evenings for "Quackery: The Dark Side of Medicine." The first tour of its kind, it explores outrageous and deadly medical treatments from back in the day.

DIVE INTO PIRATE CULTURE
AT THE PIRATE AND SHIPWRECK MUSEUMS

It's not unusual to see pirates carousing around downtown singing a chantey or two. Get up close and personal with them—if you dare.

The St. Augustine Pirate & Treasure Museum hosts a unique collection of authentic pirate artifacts that are mixed with interactive technology to take visitors through the Golden Age of Piracy. Kids always ask if the adventure includes "good" pirates or "bad" pirates. Considering some of the pirates attacked St. Augustine in the 17th century, it's assumed we're talking about bad pirates here! Owner Pat Croce (who is a local legend in my original hometown of Philadelphia) has been collecting pirate "stuff" since he was a kid. His pirate booty was once housed in Key West before coming to St. Augustine.

The St. Augustine Shipwreck Museum & Gallery showcases treasures and artifacts as well as deep-sea displays and hands-on experiences. Featured shipwrecks include the world's earliest intact shipwreck—found at the bottom of the Black Sea—and the 19th-century cargo vessel found off St. Augustine's Crescent Beach in November 2020.

The St. Augustine Pirate
& Treasure Museum
12 S Castillo Dr., 904-819-1444
thepiratemuseum.com

St. Augustine Shipwreck Museum
46 Charlotte St., 904-217-0655
staugustinemuseum.com

DISCOVER A BEST-KEPT SECRET AT THE GOVERNOR'S HOUSE CULTURAL CENTER AND MUSEUM

Since 1598, this historic site has been serving the city, first as administrative headquarters and then as a home for colonial governors. In 1821, it became a courthouse and then the capitol building for the Territory of Florida. In 1937 it became a post office, and in 1959 the St. Augustine Historical Restoration and Preservation Commission took over the building to ensure it could be protected. Now, the University of Florida owns it, and it's called the Governor's House Cultural Center and Museum.

Part of the building's coquina walls date back to St. Augustine's first Spanish colonial period, making them part of the art and artifact collection. "The House" is open to the public, with the free museum hosting annual rotating exhibits. It's located directly across the street from the Plaza de la Constitución and is still one of the best-kept secrets in St. Augustine.

48 King St., 904-825-5034
staugustine.ufl.edu/visit.html

JUMP IN THE BOX
ON FIRST FRIDAYS

Every first Friday from 5 to 9 p.m., more than 30 participating art galleries open their doors and welcome art lovers, serving wine and hosting local musicians in their community spaces. Often, featured artists are on-site to chat about their work, too. The Art Galleries of St. Augustine (staaa.org/art-galleries-of-st-augustine) hosts the citywide event.

The party always seems to start at Art Box 137 on King Street. As a "mixed-use destination gallery and creative space" that promotes positivity and creativity, Art Box is an eclectic spot where artists, locals, and visitors gather to inspire each other, to drink wine, hear live music, and to enjoy the current exhibits. Besides being a key spot on First Fridays, Art Box has also hosted plays, improv shows, independent films, talks, and other events for the community's residents and guests to enjoy. It's a wonderful place to shop for a unique piece of St. Augustine to take home, too.

Art Box 137
137 King St., 904-704-1121
artbox-137.com

TIP

Aviles Street is the oldest street in the country and is St. Augustine's original artist district. It's closed to traffic on First Fridays.

OTHER FEATURED FIRST FRIDAY ART GALLERIES

HISTORIC ART DISTRICT

Joel Bagnal, Goldsmith
11C Aviles, St., 904-614-4706
joelbagnalgoldsmith.com

PAStA Fine Art Gallery
214 Charlotte St., 904-824-0251
pastagalleryart.com

Plum Gallery
10 Aviles St., 904-825-0069
plumartgallery.com

SAN SEBASTIAN DISTRICT

Alma Ramirez Gallery
134 Riberia St., #101, 904-553-7986
alma-ramirez.com

Butterfield Garage Art Gallery
137 King St., 904-825-4577
butterfieldgarage.com

ANASTASIA ISLAND DISTRICT

High Tide Gallery
850 Anastasia Blvd., 904-315-6690
thehightidegallery.com

The Art Studio of St. Augustine Beach
370A A1A Beach Blvd., St. Augustine Beach, 904-295-4428
beachartstudio.org

W.B. Tatter Studio Gallery
806 Anastasia Blvd., 904-687-8423
wbtattergallery.com

76

APPRECIATE A HAPPY ACCIDENT
AT THE ALMA RAMIREZ GALLERY

Originally from Mexico, Alma Ramirez brought her contemporary art to St. Augustine and now runs the Alma Ramirez Gallery in Lincolnville. The contemporary abstract art inspired by nature and water is unique because of a happy accident. In 2014, Ramirez had distorted images on her camera after accidentally dropping it into the water. Those images became her new lens for viewing the world. The pixelated layering technique has become her artistic signature and her life philosophy as well. The pixelated images of boats, waterways, horizons, and florals remind us that new paths often pop up because of life's broken moments.

Ramirez says, "I recite the poetry of nature—sounds of the ocean, smells in the air, dappled light on the water, colors warmed by the sun—painting arrangements of tones and shapes that speak of emotions, beauty, and peace."

The Alma Ramirez Gallery participates in the First Friday Artwalk.

134 Riberia St., #101, 904-553-7986
alma-ramirez.com

77

BE SURPRISED
AT THE VISITOR INFORMATION CENTER

The St. Augustine and St. Johns County Visitor Information Center (VIC) is more than an information desk, restroom, and gift shop.

Outside the VIC is a fountain that was a gift from Aviles, Spain. It's a replica of one in Aviles known as the *Fuentos de los Caños de San Francisco* and features six faces with water pouring from their mouths. It's a photo opp that can't be missed.

The Old Spanish Trail (OST) ran from San Diego to St. Augustine. Construction began in 1915, and the trail officially opened in 1929. The name is an homage to Spanish heritage and southern missions. The OST follows what became US Highway 80 in the Southwest and US Highway 90 in the South. The "zero" milestone marking the end of the trail is located next to the VIC.

10 S Castillo Dr., 904-825-1000
citystaug.com/618/visitor-information-center

FUN FACT

The spherical "zero" monument is made of St. Augustine coquina—rock formed from seashells.

MEET ST. AUGUSTINE'S OLDEST RESIDENT

AT VILLA 1565

A short walk north from historic downtown is the Villa 1565 courtyard. In the center of the courtyard is St. Augustine's oldest resident, the "Old Senator"—a 650-plus-year-old live oak tree. That means the Old Senator was in St. Augustine more than a century before Ponce de Leon got here! If only it could talk—imagine the stories it could tell!

Old Senator's girth measures more than 21 feet, and he's more than 56 feet tall. If trees had to wear clothes, he'd be shopping at the big-and-tall store! He's pretty rad any time of year, but in the winter, he's dressed in his holiday finest as part of the Nights of Lights display.

His house—Villa 1565—is a charming hotel with Spanish architecture, a coquina exterior, and a lovely courtyard with the Old Senator in the middle of it. Selfies are encouraged here!

TIP

Coquina, rock made from seashells, was used in St. Augustine construction as early as 1598, starting a building tradition.

VISIT ONE OF SEVEN LOVE TREES

The coastal Florida climate is responsible for the "love tree"—two separate trees growing in, on, and through each other. Local lore says that lovers kissing beneath one of these trees will have a lifetime of romance together. Want to cast a love spell?

The former Love Tree Cottage yard
6 Cordova St.

Villa 1565 Hotel parking lot
137 San Marco Ave.

Bridge Street near the Cathedral Parish School
259 St. George St.

The Mission Nombre de Dios grounds
101 San Marco Ave.

At a Lincolnville historic house
294 St. George St.

Next to Ameris Bank
790 N Ponce de Leon Blvd.

At the Council on Aging's grounds
180 Marine St.

79

CELEBRATE HISTORIC WOMEN

AT THE XIMENEZ-FATIO HOUSE MUSEUM

In 1798, Don Andrés Ximenez built a coquina house for his wife Juana Pellicer and their children. In 1830, Margaret Cook bought it and turned it into a boarding house. Sarah Petty Anderson then bought it and lived there for 15 years with Louisa Fatio as the manager. In 1855, Louisa Fatio bought it and maintained it as a boarding house for almost 25 years. It remained in Louisa's family until 1939, when the National Society of the Colonial Dames of America in the State of Florida purchased the property, restoring and furnishing it to create a historic house museum. Today it's still owned and operated by (mostly) women.

Visit during the day to experience 220 years of history and learn how early Floridians created a new industry: tourism.

Visit after dark for A Night Among Ghosts—a professional paranormal investigation hosted by a local investigator.

20 Aviles St., 904-829-3575
ximenezfatiohouse.org

PRETEND TO BE ROYALTY
AT THE VILLA ZORAYDA MUSEUM

An architectural masterpiece built by Bostonian Franklin Smith in 1883, the Villa Zorayda was built at one-tenth of the scale of the Moorish castle, the Alhambra, in Granada, Spain. The Gilded Age home was Smith's winter retreat and was constructed from a mixture of concrete and crushed coquina shells. It began the Moorish Spanish Revival style of architecture that is seen throughout the city, and its innovative construction method became the norm at the turn of the 19th century, with Villa Zorayda leading the way.

Listed on the National Register of Historic Places, the museum hosts a collection of antiques and fine art as well as the "Sacred Cat Rug," an Egyptian rug more than 2,400 years old made of ancient cat hair from felines who roamed around the Nile River.

83 King St., 904-829-9887
villazorayda.com

81

CELEBRATE EASTER WEEK IN HISTORIC DOWNTOWN ST. AUGUSTINE

Performed every year during Easter week, the Royal Knighting Ceremony honors locals for their good civic deeds by having the royal family "knight" them. The "St. Augustine Royal Family" represents Spain's Royal Family of 1672—the year the Castillo de San Marcos was commissioned—with a king, queen, and princess. The royal family also leads the Easter parade.

The Easter parade is the second oldest in the country—it's been running annually in St. Augustine since 1956. Spectators line the historic downtown streets to see the St. Augustine Royal Family, bands, parade floats, pirates, drill teams, clowns, storm troopers (not kidding), carriage horses, and the Easter Bunny.

The Easter Promenade is all about outrageous Easter bonnets! Awards are presented in various categories and prizes are distributed at the end of the judging.

visitstaugustine.com/topics/easter

82

HAVE AN IMMERSIVE EXPERIENCE AT THE OLDEST STORE MUSEUM

The Oldest Store Museum re-creates St. Augustine's C. F. Hamblen store—the original general store. The transformation from store to museum took more than three years as three and a half stories of antiques were removed from the store and placed into a climate-controlled facility to protect and preserve history. Then thousands of pieces of 19th- and early 20th-century items from the original store were cataloged while developing the museum. The historians re-created the period-appropriate general store using original counters, displays, and merchandise. Today, living history tour guides play the parts of clerks and salespeople demonstrating the latest inventions for turn-of-the-century "modern" living including unicycles, goat-powered washing machines, collars and corsets, and all sorts of tonics and elixirs, including worm syrup. It's an immersive experience filled with tchotchkes, rusty and weathered cans, medicine bottles, and a treasure trove of goods and hardware from "the olden days."

167 San Marco Ave., 904-829-3800
trolleytours.com/st-augustine/oldest-store-museum

83

FIND PEACE ON EARTH
AT CASTLE OTTTIS

Just off A1A, five miles north of historic downtown, sits Castle Otttis (with three ts). Ottis Sadler and Rusty Ickes built the castle between 1984 and 1988 to be a landscape sculpture based on 1,000-year-old Irish castles. Sadler and Ickes did all the masonry—without any help from paid labor or even family members. When the walls were high enough to be noticed by passersby, they got bad news—they needed a permit. Due to a government clerical error with the permit, the building in progress was declared as a garage—built of concrete blocks, steel rods, and poured concrete that weighed about seven million pounds—with ramparts and 88 window openings, all without glass. Not only did this leave the interior exposed to the elements, but it also made for the strangest "garage" in St. Augustine.

Lee Carpenter created the interior, under guidance from Catholic historians, to evoke an Irish abbey feel. Between 1988 and 1991, he built eight staircases, an altar, a pulpit, a choir loft, a bishop's chair, and pews.

The result is a majestic stone castle to express artistic and spiritual devotion. In 1992, the American Institute of Architects recognized Castle Otttis as a new landmark.

103 3rd St.
castleotttis.com

TIP
Castle Otttis is not open to the public,
but it's worth a drive by while cruising the
scenic coastal byway.

Market baskets on display at Zora Bora Gallery on Cuna Street in historic downtown.

SHOPPING AND FASHION

84

BE THE BEE'S KNEES
AT STUBBEES

Everyone loves a local success story, and this one is a perfect example. Founded by Justin Stubblefield (hence the name, "Stubbees"), the business started when Justin sold his honey at the St. Augustine Amphitheatre Farmers Market. Justin's appreciation of bees—and his knowledge of honey—led to a successful online business. In 2018, the Stubbees store opened, providing the town with small-batch honey food items as well as botanically inspired apothecary and skin-care products—all made with natural ingredients, of course.

Find raw honey, bourbon-infused honey, mango habanero–infused honey, comb honey, and raw creamed honey flavored with cinnamon, vanilla bean, and orange zest. Pick up shaving cream, face cleaners, body soaps, throat spray, dietary supplements, facial scrubs, toners, note cards, clothing, and bees-wrap food storage sheets. BYO shopping bag.

Stubbees supports honeybee conservation and sources honey from American beekeepers of all backgrounds.

Hive & Homestead by Stubbees
Sells honey products
as well as home gift items
92 Charlotte St., 904-679-4966

Stubbees Honey + APothecary
Specializes in honey products
made by locally raised bees
102 St. George St., 904-679-4966

stubbees.com

MOONWALK OVER
TO MUSIC MATTERS REMIXED

There is something soothing about an old-fashioned record store. Spend a rainy day browsing the aisles as if it's a treasure hunt with surprise booty waiting to be discovered.

Since 1989, Music Matters Remixed has been St. Augustine's home for new and used CDs, cassettes, records, DVDs, music accessories, and books. It also showcases hard-to-find imports from the UK, Europe, and Asia. While many music genres are represented, Music Matters is most known for its huge '80s New Wave section.

Other fun finds at Music Matters include action figures, T-shirts, posters, magazines, lava lamps, incense, stickers, turntables, guitars, ukuleles, harmonicas, keyboards, and synthesizers, as well as music accessories. With unique items ranging from $1 to $300, no one ever knows what magic awaits on a visit to Music Matters Remixed.

196 State Rd. 312, 904-824-5740
facebook.com/musicmatters89

86

CREATE MORE HAPPINESS WITH A VISIT
TO DECLARATION & CO.: THE MARKETPLACE

With a tagline that reads "clothing for everyday + gifts for everyone," Declaration & Co: The Marketplace is a darling boutique celebrating St. Augustine's creativity, fashion, gift giving, and community. Their mission is to create happiness through their products, and the Declaration & Co. team curates the shop with love.

Browse the store to discover candles, coffee and tea, baby and mama gifts, hats, jewelry, bags, books, key chains, clothing, stickers, greeting cards and stationery, glassware, and toys. There's a special line of products, the Land of Sunshine Collection, that has been designed to celebrate St. Augustine and the Sunshine State.

Declaration & Co. also hosts the annual Dashing through the Store event—a weekend-long holiday kickoff and private shopping party that supports a different local charity every year.

It's hard to visit Declaration & Co. without picking out a treat or two—or more!

63 San Marco Ave., #3257, 904-295-2476
shopdeclaration.com

ENJOY EXOTIC AND ECLECTIC SHOPPING

AT COASTAL TRADERS

Sometimes there's no time to jet off to Indonesia to shop. That's why there's Coastal Traders! This colorfully eclectic shop features fine handcrafted Indonesian furniture, home decor, clothing, accessories, and one-of-a-kind art pieces. Coastal Traders also showcases work from St. Augustine's artists, so there's always a bit of local flavor mixed in with the exotic pieces on display.

The shop has become so popular that it expanded into the space next door, making for an even bigger shopping experience for visitors and locals. The recycled boat wood furniture can be spotted in quite a few homes and businesses around town.

Coastal Traders offers a unique shopping experience in St. Augustine's Uptown neighborhood—it's like having a vacation within a vacation.

56 San Marco Ave., 904-460-2248
coastaltradersimports.com

TIP

Be sure to check out the matchbooks at the register that feature St. Augustine landmarks.

88

BE ROCK, PUNK, OR METRO MOD

AT ROCK N ROLL CIRCUS ALES & APPAREL

Occasionally there's a local treasure that's hard to define because it has so many fun offerings. Rock N Roll Circus Ales & Apparel, on Anastasia Island, is one such place. It serves as St. Augustine's one-stop shop for rock, vintage, rockabilly, punk, ska, and retro mod clothing—and it's also a live music venue and bar.

With clothing arriving regularly from Liverpool, Rock N Roll Circus features band T-shirts and socks, go-go boots, and kitten sunglasses. There are also cowboy boots, shirts, and hats, as well as stickers, flower-power jumpsuits, and vintage dresses.

Rock N Roll Circus serves canned drinks at the front counter—both alcoholic and nonalcoholic—so enjoy a cold one while browsing. On the weekends, Rock N Roll Circus opens the back room to live local bands.

112 Anastasia Blvd., 570-604-5029

89

GET A ONE-OF-A-KIND T-SHIRT
AT MATERIALISTIC

Materialistic, an uptown shop offering an eclectic and entertaining mix of merchandise, carries novelty socks, silly air fresheners, and funny magnets. There's also fun jewelry, humorous enamel pins, quirky animal masks, snarky oven mitts, gift mugs, and fashion sunglasses.

Materialistic also has books for kids and grown-ups. Forgot to pack a beach read? Pick one up while also grabbing a super silly souvenir.

Among the most iconic merchandise at Materialistic are the St. Augustine screen-print T-shirts. The shirts feature unique designs such as the town's coordinates, sailboats, nautical flags, and way more, that can't be found anywhere else. There are short- and long-sleeve T-shirts available for men, women, and children.

For a small shop, Materialistic offers a big—and fun—shopping experience.

76B San Marco Ave., 904-342-2487

90

PLEASE TOUCH EVERYTHING
AT OLDE TOWNE TOYS

Feel like a kid again at Olde Towne Toys while pretending to shop for the children in the family. The shop has an eclectic collection of one-of-a-kind toys—some educational and some for all ages.

Located in what was once a house, the toy shop encourages grown-ups and kids to touch everything while wandering from room to room. The shop carries toys that teach kids to be creative while embracing the joy of learning through play. The featured brands encourage learning while also captivating the imagination.

There's an area in the shop where grown-ups can relax while kids check out the merch. The real fun is the room that houses a train table, a play kitchen, and a dollhouse for the kids to play in while the grown-ups shop.

Olde Towne Toys is the largest independent specialty toy store in St. Augustine!

300 S Ponce de Leon Blvd., 904-342-8008
oldetownetoys.com

CREATE CUSTOMIZABLE BATH PRODUCTS
AT BATH JUNKIE AND CELEBRATE AT THE TIPSY DUCK

Bath Junkie's name is no joke. Here, besides shopping for soaps, bodywashes, lotions, and bath scrubs, you can customize scents and colors for yourself, your partner, and even your dog. The shop features more than 200 scents and 18 colors to mix and match to create customizable bath luxuries!

Bath Junkie also carries organic cotton robes as well as handmade fortune-cookie glycerin soaps and bath balls.

And the fun doesn't stop there. What's a bath shop without rubber duckies? Inside Bath Junkie is the Tipsy Duck—a gathering spot for sipping themed cocktails on duck-feet bar stools. The Tipsy Duck's bar has bubbles running through it, bathtub couches, and other tubs filled with, yes, rubber duckies. Dive into the bathtubs, bins, and baskets to select a traditional or themed rubber ducky to take home.

63 Hypolita St., 904-810-2284
bathjunkiestaugustine.com

92

GLOW YOUR OWN WAY
AT HAPPY PAPPYS GLOWING BALLS

Who is Pappy? No one knows. What we do know is that this Pappy is happy, because you can't be anything but with a glowing ball from Happy Pappys Glowing Balls.

Choose the size, shape, and color, and the Happy Pappy crew will assemble it in the moment. These hanging plastic lamps are made in all shapes and colors and come with a 12-foot cord—and they are the perfect gift for anyone who loves whimsy.

Select glow balls that are stars, pineapples, cats, unicorns, pandas, and sea creatures. There are endless possibilities. Keep mixing and matching until the "wow" moment arrives.

There's a lot of joy coming from this tiny shop in St. Augustine's Uptown neighborhood. Keep an eye out around town to see the glowing balls in action.

76a San Marco Ave., 305-527-6128
facebook.com/happypappysglowingballs

93

REMEMBER THE WAY WE WERE
AT COOL AND COLLECTED

Take a spin through Cool and Collected, St. Augustine's home for unique vintage items in the Uptown neighborhood, and reflect on the days when we were cool. The shop is a big old house that's been converted into showrooms featuring clothing and shoes, kitchenware, furniture, art, and home decor, as well as fun novelty items from the 1930s through the 1970s.

Southern Living magazine mentioned Cool and Collected as the place to browse rattan furniture and vintage barware. It also has ceramic ashtrays, old globes, silly flamingos, Hawaiian shirts, vintage suitcases, and the list goes on. Every trip to Cool and Collected is different, and no two items are the same. It's like one big treasure chest with old-time booty waiting to go to just the right person.

67 San Marco Ave., 904-824-6113
facebook.com/coolandcollectedvintage

94

STOCK UP ON PIRATE BOOTY
AT THE PIRATE STORE

Want an authentic pirate outfit to wear on the *Black Raven* pirate ship? They got that. Want a souvenir to take home to remember St. Augustine pirate life? They got that too! The Pirate Store offers pirate novelties, collectibles, and souvenirs including pirate hats, shirts, coats, and costumes. Find hand-carved wooden signs, leather bags, and pirate conversation pieces. They even have pirate-themed jewelry, including bracelets, necklaces, and rings.

The Pirate Store also works with craftspeople and seamstresses to provide guests with authentic reenactment clothing to reflect the Golden Age of Piracy. The store's "captain" works with first-time buccaneers, professional reenactors, live-action role-playing gamers, Renaissance Faire folks, pirate krewes, and pirate-themed wedding planners to help design unique personas.

It's like entering another world—one that is totally unique to St. Augustine.

162 St. George St., Ste. 28, 904-392-1172
pirate4.life

FEEL THE SPIRIT OF THE SEA AT SEA SPIRITS GALLERY & GIFTS

Love the ocean hues? Then step into Sea Spirits Gallery & Gifts. A fine-art appraiser and archeologist, gallery owner Victoria Golden has curated a space filled with paintings, sculptures, blown glass, unique decor, artisan jewelry, nautical items, and handcrafted gifts inspired by the sea. The room's aquas, blues, and greens feel like the spirit of the sea is right there in the gallery.

Local and international artists have a hand in creating the designer jewelry featured at Sea Spirits. Classic and unusual pieces—made from ancient Roman glass, sea glass, agate, turquoise, opal, and nautilus shell—are on display in sterling silver and gold settings. Some of the Roman glass is 2,000 years old and is stunning—especially as pieces of jewelry.

210 St. George St., Ste. C-2, 904-679-3811
seaspiritsgallery.com

TIP

Sea Spirits Gallery and sister gallery next door, Lost Art Gallery, both participate in the First Friday Artwalk.

MAKE YOUR SWEET TOOTH HAPPY

AT PASSPORT SWEETS AND CARNIVAL SWEETS

St. Augustine is filled with an abundance of sweets, whether its ice cream, cookies, cakes, cupcakes, macarons, or candy.

Have an adventurous sweet tooth? Travel around the world via Passport Sweets in historic downtown. Taste the sweet side of faraway places without leaving the heart of St. Augustine by stocking up on Japanese, European, and Latin American candy.

Equally fun with a completely different spin on candy is Carnival Sweets. Located about 10 minutes south of the historic center, Carnival Sweets transports guests to a forgotten era via an old-time candy shop. This is the place to go for families traveling together. It makes people from 5 to 95 happy by serving funnel cakes, gourmet popcorn, and shaved ice as well as shelves and shelves of candy in a vintage setting. The old-time candy shop also serves carnival treats such as candied apples and fried Oreos.

Passport Sweets
100 St. George St., Ste. C (inside the Spanish Plaza), 904-679-5292
passportsweets.com

Carnival Sweets
288 FL-312 (inside the Riverside Center), 904-342-8041
carnivalsweetsstaugustine.com

97

GET A SOUVENIR TATTOO
AT INK & BARLEY TATTOOS AND BREWS

Another fun addition to the Uptown neighborhood is Ink & Barley Tattoos and Brews. Is this a tattoo studio with a craft-beer bar and a souvenir shop, or is this a craft-beer bar with a tattoo studio and a souvenir shop? Yes! When a tattoo artist and a beer enthusiast marry and go into business together, this is what you have—a creative space for locals and visitors to gather to discuss tattoo art and design while enjoying a cold one . . . and maybe even taking a souvenir home (it could be something from the shop, or an actual tattoo).

Not sure if it's the place to be? Check out their website to see which guest tattoo artists are visiting and the list of rotating taps, too. Or better yet, don't prepare and just show up. Enjoy the artists, enjoy the beer, enjoy the socializing, and enjoy the souvenirs. And then ask yourself, "Why doesn't my city have a place like this?"

35 San Marco Ave., 904-599-2965
inkandbarley.com

BRING HOME A DATIL PEPPER PLANT
FROM MAGGIE'S HERB FARM

A licensed nursery 20 miles west of downtown on County Road 13 by the St. Johns River, Maggie's Herb Farm has been a staple in the community since 1983. Owner, herbalist, and artist Dora Baker (no, she's not named Maggie) worked in clinical herb settings using Ayurvedic, Chinese, and Western herbalism—she even ran herbal programs for Walt Disney World and EPCOT.

Purchase unusual varieties of herb plants, perennials for butterfly or hummingbird gardens, nectar and fruit plants, and the local delicacy, the datil pepper plant—both hot and sweet.

The gift shop has birdhouses, owner-designed T-shirts, herb books, farm honey, jams, datil-pepper mustard, homemade soaps, pottery, sage, and natural bug repellants.

Maggie's Herb Farm also hosts events such as yoga classes and herb-growing workshops.

11400 County Rd. 13 N, 904-829-0722
maggiesherbfarm.com

DRINK, PLAY, SHOP—AND EAT PIE

AT SPINSTER ABBOTT'S

Is Spinster Abbott's a neighborhood market or a neighborhood bar? Both! Located in St. Augustine's walkable Uptown neighborhood, "Spinster's" carries locally sourced groceries, household basics, coffee, beer, and wine as well as grab-and-go bites. It's a great place to pick up items for a beach, park, or boat picnic. It's an even better place to hang out before or after shopping, as the taproom is like a little secret third space—a place to go to spend time with people you don't see at work or at home. The bodega and the bar are decorated with nostalgic colors as well as vintage art and furniture, giving it an old-fashioned five-and-dime-shop-meets-Prohibition-speakeasy vibe.

And the pies! The Spinster team hits a home run with modern southern hospitality—because of the pies.

No matter the reason for visiting, Old Florida charm mixed with an eclectic retro ambiance will be there to greet you with a local beer and a slice of pie!

61 San Marco Ave., 904-201-9959
spinsterabbotts.com

TIP

Spinster Abbott's hosts game nights and live music nights, too.

SHOP ÜBERLOCAL
AT ST. AUGUSTINE'S MARKETS

There are a few places to secure organic fresh produce, handmade arts and crafts, baked goods, plants from local farms, fresh-caught seafood, cheeses, and baked good while listening to local musicians and eating from food trucks. Each market is like a little street party, whether it's next to the ocean or the state park.

The granddaddy of them all is the Saturday St. Augustine Amphitheatre Farmers Market. Here locals and visitors gather to enjoy local music, good food, fun treats, and artisan creations. Enjoy the handmade delicacies and crafts under the big old oak trees and stock up on goodies for the vacation home and the "home" home. It's a great way to shop, eat, drink, and listen local. It's also a great way to put together a picnic lunch for the beach or for one of the local state parks.

The St. Augustine
Amphitheatre Farmers Market
Saturdays 8:30 a.m. to 12:30 p.m.

The St. Augustine Amphitheatre
1340C A1A S, 904-209-3746
theamp.com/farmers-market

The St. Augustine Amphitheatre Night Market
Select Tuesdays throughout the year from 5 p.m. to 9 p.m.

TIP

Arrive early for better parking options and when vendors have full tables of merchandise.

OTHER LOCAL MARKETS

The Farmers Market at the St. Johns County Pier
Every Wednesday 8 a.m. to noon

Vilano Beach Artisan Market at Vilano Town
Third Saturday of the month from 4 p.m. to 8 p.m.

visitstaugustine.com/article/st-augustines-local-farmers-markets

ACTIVITIES
BY SEASON

SPRING

SUMMER

FALL

WINTER

SUGGESTED ITINERARIES

TASTES OF ST. AUGUSTINE

FAMILY AFFAIR

ACTIVE ADVENTURER

HISTORY LESSONS

TAKE IN THE ARTS

DRINK IT IN

THE WILD SIDE

TOURS AND MORE

UNIQUELY ST. AUGUSTINE

GET OUTSIDE

AROUND THE WORLD

ME TIME

INDEX